Comedy and Society
from Congreve to Fielding

STANFORD STUDIES IN
LANGUAGE AND LITERATURE, XIX

Comedy and Society
from Congreve to Fielding

JOHN LOFTIS

STANFORD UNIVERSITY PRESS
STANFORD, CALIFORNIA

STANFORD UNIVERSITY PRESS
STANFORD, CALIFORNIA

© 1959 BY THE BOARD OF TRUSTEES OF THE
LELAND STANFORD JUNIOR UNIVERSITY

PRINTED IN THE UNITED STATES OF AMERICA

Original edition 1959
Reprinted 1960, 1966

For
LOUIS LANDA

Preface

The change in comedy's social orientation that occurred in the early eighteenth century has always been recognized in broad outline. Indeed, generalizations about the impact of the "middle class" upon comedy have provided the most venerable platitudes in college courses in literature. But the generalizations have remained platitudes—true, perhaps, but lacking precision and specific content. It is my hope that this book will supply both.

The period from Congreve to Fielding offers special advantages for a study of the interaction of comedy and society. For one thing, the interaction was lively: comedy and society underwent parallel and related changes. The dramatists are intensely preoccupied with the contemporary scene, and above all with social relationships exacerbated by the increase in the wealth of businessmen. The period also offers a methodological advantage in that the number of comedies first produced, though large, is not too large for exhaustive study. I have not been compelled to depend on a sampling, but rather have been able to examine virtually all of them.

Because of the convention that gives drama life—that the dramatist does not speak in his own person, nor, if he is skilled, in that of one of his characters, but rather through the whole of his dramatic situation—the interpretation of the ideas latent in a play can be a hazardous enterprise. When the playwright is successful, it is difficult to distinguish the expression of ideas from dramatic expediency; when he is less skillful, the interpretation can be more positive. Yet even the most unlearned, unsophisticated playwright does not escape the conditioning effects of literary tradition and of the technical requirements of his literary medium. The relationship between drama and contemporary life, then, is not direct but oblique. Quite steadily in this book I am concerned with the interaction of dramatic formalism and social forces.

I have avoided biographical comment except in rare cases in which it has some special relevance. Since I am working with a large number of dramatists, any extended discussion of their lives would obscure the themes that I am concerned to emphasize. And, in fact, for most of them biographical detail does not exist.

I have sought to avoid nineteenth- and twentieth-century conceptions of the nature of social classes and of the relationships between them, referring instead to the large body of early-eighteenth-century social commentary. If Swift and Addison establish the terms of my exposition of the antagonism between the landed and the moneyed interests, I can be confident that I am not introducing alien categories from a later time. I have, above all, attempted to avoid the omnibus phrase "the middle class," on the grounds that it is imprecise and, for modern readers, evaluative rather than merely descriptive.

I have adopted the customary modern compromise in using the eighteenth-century calendar, following eighteenth-century dates except that I consider a year as beginning on January 1. The years that I give for plays are those in which the plays were first made public, either in print or on the stage.

My obligations are out of proportion to the length of this book. First of all, I thank my wife and daughters for their assistance as well as their tolerance. To the Ford Foundation I am indebted for a year's respite from teaching during which I wrote most of the book. The editors of *Modern Philology* and of the *Huntington Library Quarterly* have kindly permitted me to use several short passages that I published earlier. I have profited from the help of the editorial department of the Stanford University Press. Mr. John S. Bullen prepared the Index; Mr. George A. Tsongas prepared the line drawing illustrating the growth of London. My colleagues Professors Robert W. Ackerman, Malcolm Goldstein, Richard Foster Jones, David Levin, George F. Sensabaugh, and Virgil K. Whitaker have provided counsel and assistance, in several instances time-consuming assistance. To my former colleagues at UCLA, Professors Hugh G. Dick, John Harrington Smith, and H. T. Swedenberg, Jr., I remain in debt for substantial help in the earlier stages of my work. I am proud to be able to say that I discussed the preliminary plan for this book with the late Edward Niles Hooker, my association with whom I count a special privilege. And finally I acknowledge a large and continuing intellectual debt to Professor Louis A. Landa, to whom this book is dedicated.

JOHN LOFTIS

Stanford, California
May 25, 1959

Contents

ONE   *Introduction*   I

TWO   *Social Rivalry and Critical Controversy*   20

THREE   *The Survival of the Restoration Stereo-*
types, 1693–1710   43

FOUR   *The End of the War and Change in*
Comedy, 1710–1728   77

FIVE   *The Displacement of the Restoration*
Tradition, 1728–1737   101

SIX   *The Decline of Drama*   133

Notes   139

Index   149

Comedy and Society
from Congreve to Fielding

Introduction

English comedy of the early eighteenth century reveals an intense preoccupation with the social results of economic change—and for good reasons. At the threshold of her two centuries of European supremacy, England enjoyed a prosperity that had been made possible by the endeavors of English merchants. Yet only in the late seventeenth and early eighteenth centuries was a traditional disdain for the merchants largely suppressed: the merchants only then came to social maturity. The many efforts at their social rehabilitation so prominent in early-eighteenth-century drama (in the plays, say, of Steele and Lillo), had their origin in controversy; they would not have appeared had there not been an active opposition. The incongruity of the merchants' prominence in the nation's economy compared with the subordinate role to which they had long been assigned provided a tension that dominates the social relationships of comedy.

Most of the important writers of the early eighteenth century, and not dramatists only, gave abundant evidence that they were aware of a modification in the structure of society; and most of them expressed either approval or disapproval. The lines were firmly drawn. Pope and Swift, the most distinguished writers of the age, were socially conservative. In *The Rape of the Lock*, Pope alludes, but no more than alludes, to the commercial society that surrounds Belinda's aristocratic circle, touching by innuendo a theme that becomes dominant in his satires, notably his *Imitations of Horace* and his *Epistles to Several Persons*. The third and fourth *Epistles* (or *Moral Essays*) will illustrate my point. Both are concerned with "the Use of Riches": the third, addressed to Lord Bathurst, chiefly with avarice, especially as practiced by moneyed men of the City; and the fourth, addressed to Lord Burlington, with prodigality, especially as exhibited in the bad taste of the newly rich who were acquiring country estates. A contrast in these poems is established between the aristocrats of long standing, the Bathursts and the Burlingtons, who with good taste follow the golden mean, and the parvenus, the Sir Balaams from the City, who commit excesses either of avarice or of prodigality. The corruption of Walpole's England, as Pope saw it and denounced it in many poems, was associated with the ascendancy of the moneyed men over the landed. Swift's attachment to the older social order was fully as strong. "I ever abominated that scheme of politicks," he wrote, "(now about thirty years old) of setting up a mony'd Interest in opposition to the landed. For, I conceived, there could not be a truer maxim in our government than this, That the possessors of the soil are the best judges of what is for the advantage of the kingdom."[1] A conservative by settled conviction, in social instincts as in literary tastes, he states comprehensively in his political writings of the last years of Queen Anne the political philosophy underlying the conservative position. It is unnecessary to mention other writers preoccupied with the conflict between the landed and the moneyed interests; almost all of them were.

Early-eighteenth-century plays include many forthright discussions of the importance of merchants and of trade to the nation. But to isolate the impact of the moneyed class upon the drama, it is not enough to cite these passages, however impressive their number and prominence. Rather, it is in the more elusive, because more inward, fact of changed dramatic values, reflecting changed social values, that the more meaningful impress of the altered social organization on the drama and, indeed, on all departments of literature is to be sought. The social assumptions of dramatists, then as always, conditioned the choice of subject, the direction assumed by dramatic satire, and frequently the course of dramatic action. The comedies of Congreve could be written only by one who accepted without major reservation the social and political assumptions of the aristocratic society based on land. At the other extreme, Lillo's treatment of merchant characters was conditioned by his conviction, largely a social conviction, that they possess the dignity requisite for high literary art.

The presence of irony complicates, but does not fundamentally alter, the problem of the social relationships exhibited in the drama. In nearly all Restoration comedy some irony appears, though it is scarcely so pervasive as the dramatists replying to Jeremy Collier's criticism of the stage seemed to think it was; and yet few seventeenth-century dramatists convey an ironic awareness of the limitations of then current aristocratic assumptions. But after the turn of the century—and after the Collier controversy coincident with it—a more critical note appears. A nondramatic poem, Pope's *Rape of the Lock*, provides perhaps our finest literary example of the use of irony to suggest—on the surface, in the tradition of the comedy of manners—that the ostensible values governing the action of the fictional lords and ladies are not the values that obtain in life. The older social values and the new are held in neat suspension by Pope's irony. So also, though with less skill, in many contemporary comedies by William Burnaby, Thomas Baker, Richard Steele, and Susannah Centlivre, among others.

Comedy could not record the society of the late seventeenth and early eighteenth centuries without itself undergoing changes so pronounced as to constitute the extinction of the Restoration tradition, if we think of that tradition as concentrating upon wittily ironic social criticism and the interactions of a group of traditional characters, character relationships, and plot situations. The "literary fallacy" implicit in the social judgments of Restoration comedy was eliminated by well-defined stages. During the first years of the eighteenth century, the best dramatists held firmly in their satirical judgments on class relationships to evaluations not unlike those of the first generation after the Restoration. However, certain lesser yet still competent dramatists were moving away from these evaluations even at the turn of the century. After 1710, and notably after the debates preliminary to the Treaty of Utrecht, the better dramatists reversed their judgments, openly espousing the claims of the merchants, whereas the obscure dramatists continued to rely on the older satirical patterns. And after 1728, when political debate entered drama with *The Beggar's Opera*, the older character stereotypes and the accompanying satirical judgments either disappeared or were radically altered.

Characters in early-eighteenth-century plays are, with few exceptions, acutely aware of social distinctions. Yet in contemporary life the barriers between the classes, though they seem substantial by modern egalitarian standards, were not firm. Many younger sons of aristocratic families entered "trade"; many wealthy "merchants" bought land and acquired the perquisites (and in time the prestige) of the landed gentry; there was much intermarriage between the families of merchants and those of gentlemen. Even the terms "merchant" and "trade" lacked precise meaning. " 'Merchants' in the eighteenth century meant business men, and the term was as wide as 'trade' is even now; bankers and manufacturers were included in it."[2] It is important to remember, however, that despite the occasional ambiguity of the term "merchant," there was by Queen Anne's time a clearly understood distinction between men who were financiers or traders on a more or less large scale and men who were mere shopkeepers. The eulogies of the merchant in the early eighteenth century were intended to apply not to shopkeepers but rather to large-scale traders, especially to overseas traders—to the men whom Gregory King, a contemporary observer, called "merchants and traders by sea."[3] And as the terms describing mercantile life were imprecise, so also were those describing the gentry and the peerage. In England there was no "nobility" in the Continental sense of a clearly demarked caste: the word itself was commonly used in England to designate the peerage in contrast with the gentry; but the substance of the word in the Continental sense is best exemplified by the class of English families that possessed landed estates and could employ armorial bearings, a class that included families of the gentry as well as of the peerage.[4] Yet the imprecision of social terms and of the distinctions between classes applies only to generalized discussions. Within the context of individual plays, the social meaning of class distinctions and of occupations is usually apparent, just as in life it must nearly always have been.

There had long been in England some movement back and forth between the gentry and the merchant class; and the growth in prosperity of the merchants in the late seventeenth and early eighteenth centuries probably accelerated the process, primarily by making marriage between the two classes more common. But there was also a growing conviction in the early eighteenth century that successful merchants were in their own right entitled to a high place in social esteem, quite apart from their ability to transform themselves into "gentlemen" by marriage or the purchase of land. It was becoming unnecessary to cease being a merchant in order to become a gentleman. Steele certainly speaks through his dramatic character Mr. Sealand of *The Conscious Lovers* (1722) in a famous pronouncement on the subject (IV): "We Merchants are a Species of Gentry, that have grown into the World this last Century, and are as honourable, and almost as useful, as you landed Folks, that have always thought yourselves so much above us." The defiant note here is echoed widely through early-eighteenth-century literature. Merchants, in both life and literature, were in increasing numbers refusing to be bound by the conception of the "citizen." On the other hand, landowning families were becoming increasingly involved in joint-stock companies. Stockjobbing, Defoe wrote in 1724, "is so vast in its extent, that almost all the men of substance in England are more or less concerned in it."[5] The development of opportunities for safe and profitable commercial investment attracted money from the landowners as well as the merchants, though the landowning families still derived much the largest part of their income from their tenant farmers (many of them having also supplementary incomes from urban and mining properties).[6]

The commercial changes did not all contribute to a closer identification of the interests of landowners and merchants. If many of the gentry and the nobility were making investments in the public funds or in private stock companies, perhaps fewer rich merchants than earlier were investing their surplus money in land since an attractive alternative investment was available. H. J. Habakkuk describes some of the social implications of the new market for investment:

A mortgage on a large estate was the nearest approach to a first-class security which the seventeenth century knew until the foundation of the National Debt. At the end of the century an immense new field of investment was opened by government borrowing— investment at once safe and lucrative. . . . The merchant who wanted a profitable investment for any surplus not absorbed in trade could lend to the government. The land still retained its attractiveness as the most stable of all investments, especially after the South Sea crash, but to an increasing extent the merchant, who in 1640 might have left money in his will to be laid out in land and the rents settled on his children, in the early eighteenth century directed that such money be used to invest in the Funds.

This rapid extension in the field of investment explains many of the changes in the nature of the purchasers of land. Those people bought land who were peculiarly susceptible to considerations of social prestige and political power. Among them were a few large merchants, mainly chairmen of the East India Company, who went in for politics; but most of the newcomers were either connected in some way with government or were judges, who desired to have that significance in society which only the possession of land could give.[7]

Affluent merchants in the early eighteenth century, then, were not forced into a rivalry with the gentry by the necessity of investing in land as they were a century earlier. Moneyed men had no compelling economic reason to convert themselves into "landed" men. This fact probably had something to do with the merchants' insistence, depicted in the drama, that they be regarded as "a species of gentry."

Our best source of information about the relative economic position of the merchants and the gentry is Gregory King's well-known statistical estimate, computed about 1696 with reference to 1688. King's figures pertain to the whole of England, which was still predominantly agricultural; in London, of course, where the theaters were, there were far more and far richer merchants than in the country as a whole. There were 30,000 persons, King estimated, in the families of "esquires," each family, on the average, with an annual income of £450; 96,000 persons in the families of "gentlemen," each family with £280; 16,000 persons in the families of eminent "merchants and traders by sea," each family with £400; and 48,000 persons in the families of lesser "merchants and traders by sea," each family with £200.[8] These figures, it must be recalled, are for 1688; the economic position of the merchants improved markedly during the early eighteenth century.

The affluence of Gregory King's eminent and lesser merchants depended to a large extent on London's vigorous foreign trade. The volume of foreign trade, import and export, increased during the later seventeenth century, not so fast perhaps as historians formerly assumed, but substantially. It has been estimated that "imports increased by just a third, and exports by rather more than half, in the period 1663–1701, the faster growth of exports being due to the growth of the re-

export trade from the negligible proportions of the 1630's."[9]
It was in fact the very rapid expansion of the re-export trade
(especially the transshipment of colonial goods) that was the
most striking aspect of foreign trade in the later seventeenth
century; and it was characteristic of the large re-export trade
that it required relatively little investment in new industry in
comparison with the investment required for financing the
trade itself, much of it tied up in long ocean voyages. Trade
increased much more than industry, partly because England
was increasingly acting as intermediary between the American
colonies and European and Asiatic markets. This fact helps
to explain why the merchants, above all the London merchants
who controlled most of the shipping, found themselves in a
highly favorable economic position.

In the first decade of the eighteenth century the English
economy was compelled to bear the load of a foreign war, a
costly war by current standards, though eminently successful.
Because of the stimulus provided to industrial activity, the war,
all things considered, probably resulted in economic gain to
the nation, just as it certainly resulted in gain to the merchants.
The demands on English manpower were too small to occasion
shortages in agriculture or industry: less than 5 per cent of the
total male population of Great Britain was mobilized, and this
percentage included released prisoners and colonists. The
British navy, already supreme, made it possible for merchants
to reach their overseas markets and to acquire some new ones
at the expense of France and Holland. There was much gov-
ernment-stimulated industrial activity—in shipbuilding, in
metal works, in textiles—which in turn encouraged the production and sale of consumer goods. There seems even to have
been a rise in the production of consumer goods during the war.
The demands of war fostered, as always, technical advancement, including important inventions in basic industries. All of
these gains were in part offset by expenses (which had to be met
by heavy taxation), by some industrial dislocations, and even
by periods of depression in trade; but the net economic effect
of the war was probably favorable.[10]

Walpole, in his twenty-one years as first minister, had conspicuous success with an economic policy in which the encouragement of trade was a major objective. He understood the

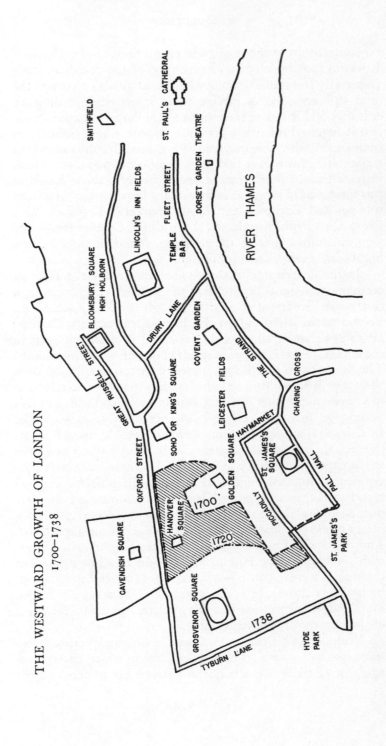

THE WESTWARD GROWTH OF LONDON
1700–1738

importance of industry and trade, and he used the resources of government, notably the import and export duties, to turn them in the most profitable directions. He consistently employed the tariffs, not to raise money, but rather to improve England's position in trade. His famous excise scheme of 1733, which occasioned a powerful and successful resistance from his political opponents, was indeed essentially designed to improve the machinery for administering the tariffs. Although a mercantilist in economic theory—he lived, after all, a generation before Adam Smith's *Wealth of Nations*—he accepted some of the principles of free trade, to the advantage of England and the London merchants. During his years in office, the colonial trade increased strikingly and·nearly all branches of commercial and industrial activity improved.[11] The merchants had reason to be grateful to him, whatever their position on the controversial issues of foreign and domestic policy that came late in his administration.

The mingling of merchant families and "honorable families" that is the subject of so many early-eighteenth-century comedies is in its larger outlines sufficiently obvious. But when we come to particulars, when we attempt to give specific content to the bare statement of the fact, we encounter the elusiveness of social change which renders close description difficult. But we are not without resources.

One such resource is provided by records of the growth of London, of growth in recognizable social patterns. Places of residence, then as now, conditioned families' social pretensions, and changes in place of residence consequently provide an objective means of estimating changes in social pretensions. The mingling of merchant families with "honorable families" can be traced in contemporary maps and descriptions of building operations in the great expansion of London to the fashionable northwest that occurred during the first third of the eighteenth century. The theaters, as always, were responsive to population shifts; and they found themselves, as a result of the expansion to the northwest, in possession of a large new audience, increasingly heterogeneous in taste and in background, that had to be taken into account when managerial policy was formulated.

In one of his several blasts at the managers of Drury Lane, John Dennis, writing in 1719, cautioned the managers against assuming that the crowds they attracted were in any sense a testimony to the quality of their productions:

But you will say, perhaps, that the Play-House was throng'd for eight or ten Days together at the Representation of these Comedies; perhaps so. But then, if it was so throng'd at the Representation of damn'd Plays, I hope my Ears will no more be stunn'd with the Noise of the Improvement of a general Taste, and that for the future no Consequence will be drawn from the Numbers of an Audience to their Capacity. For the very same Reason that the Builder's Trade, the Carpenters and the Joyners are so very much improv'd; for the very same Reason that so many fine Houses, so many beautiful Streets, so many stately Squares, and, as it were, whole Towns are building in your North-West Suburbs; for that very same Reason is your Theatre crowded. A Penetration that comes far short of Conjuration, may suffice to shew, that the Numbers of the Nobility and Gentry of the Town, and consequently of their Dependants, are exceedingly augmented by some great Events which have happen'd of late Years, *viz.* the Revolution, the Union with *Scotland*, the Return of our Armies from the Continent, and the King's Accession to the Crown. But as for the Improvement of a general Taste, 'tis so great a Blunder, that it could never be thought of among considerate People.[12]

The personal animus so plainly evident here, though limiting the value of Dennis's judgment of Drury Lane's artistic accomplishment, in no way limits the value of his factual observations on London building operations in relation to theater attendance. He speaks only of the nobility and gentry, but, as we shall see, the gentry were gaining recruits from the merchant class. Contemporary maps reveal the northwestward march of the fashionable to the vicinities of Hanover, Grosvenor, and Cavendish Squares, and the westward march of the theaters to the Haymarket and to Covent Garden.

John Summerson, curator of the Soane Museum and a modern authority on eighteenth-century London, has explained that building operations in London were carried on, not continuously, but in waves; and that one of the most important of these waves came immediately after the Treaty of Utrecht of 1713 and the Hanoverian accession of the following year.[13] Daniel Defoe commented in 1724 that the great and more eminent increase of buildings, in, and about the city of London, and the vast extent of ground taken in, and now become streets and noble squares of houses, by which the mass, or body of the whole, is become so infinitely great, has been generally made in our time, not only within our memory, but even within a few years.[14]

The building in the west was centered in four large areas—in Hanover, Grosvenor, and Cavendish-Harley Squares, and in the estate of the Earl of Burlington behind his house in Piccadilly—extending roughly from the site of the present Regent Street to Hyde Park. The nuclei of these building areas were provided by the town houses of the great: by the houses of a group of Whigs in Hanover Square (thus the name); of Tories in Cavendish-Harley Square, which was projected by the son of Queen Anne's minister; and of groups not differentiated by political allegiance in Grosvenor Square and in the Burlington estate.[15] Defoe, in describing the parishes of St. Giles' and St. Martin's in the Fields, provides details about the extent of the building in 1724:

The increase of the buildings here, is really a kind of prodigy; all the buildings north of Long Acre, up to the Seven Dials, all the streets, from Leicester-Fields and St. Martin's-Lane, both north and west, to the Hay-Market and Soho, and from the Hay-Market to St. James's-Street inclusive, and to the park wall; then all the buildings on the north side of the street, called Picadilly, and the road to Knight's-Bridge, and between that and the south side of Tyburn Road, including Soho-Square, Golden-Square, and now Hanover-Square, and that new city on the north side of Tyburn Road, called Cavendish-Square, and all the streets about it.[16]

Many of the new building sites were fashionable, and they attracted the increasing numbers of London families who could afford fashion, as well as the wealthy families who came up from the country.

The great building boom in the northwest, beginning about 1713, was but an accelerated manifestation of a trend that was already established. A guidebook published in 1729 for the use of foreign visitors describes the relation of the new buildings to the earlier pattern of London growth:

At the Time of the dreadful Fire in the Year 1666, there were but few Houses scattered up and down between *Temple-Bar* and *St.*

James's, which was then but a Field or Pasture-Ground; but all that vast Tract of Land has been since filled up with fine Streets, Churches, and Squares. But what we call the new Buildings, is that additional Part built within these Twenty Years, towards the Fields in the Liberty of *Westminster*, consisting of many thousand Houses, large and beautiful Streets, Squares, &c. where most of the Nobility and Gentry now live, for the Benefit of the Good Air, and where there are many fine Houses.[17]

Contemporary London maps show with sufficient precision the stages of the westward growth. Even at the turn of the century, some thirteen years before Hanover Square was laid out, the western extremity of continuous metropolitan building had already reached St. James's Palace, though the north-south dimension there was slight. Only a few city blocks of buildings extended north of Piccadilly Street; and Golden Square was in the extreme northwest. By 1720 the area north of St. James's had grown to include Hanover Square as the extremity of continuous building. Cavendish Square, though laid out, had not yet been overtaken by the metropolitan growth, and Grosvenor Square and its immediate environs were still in the future. By 1738 both Cavendish and Grosvenor Squares were entirely surrounded, and Tyburn Lane, marking the eastern boundary of Hyde Park, had become the western boundary of metropolitan London. And here for a time it was to remain; the great wave of expansion virtually stopped during the 1730's.

John Dennis, in a passage quoted, spoke of the cause of the great amount of building in the west as a series of important public events: the Revolution of 1688, the union with Scotland of 1707, the return of the English armies from the Continent after the Treaty of Utrecht in 1713, and George I's accession in 1714. These events certainly were contributing causes to the westward expansion, but we must look for still further causes. For one thing, the City proper, the traditional stronghold of the merchants and financiers, was rapidly losing importance; its interests were coming more and more to be identified with the shopkeepers, who made up the larger part of its common councilors and resident freemen, rather than with the leading business figures.[18] The historic City companies gave way in importance to the newer corporations, the South Sea

Company, the East India Company, the African Company, and the Bank of England, which, though they might be physically situated within the City, were not subject to control by the ancient City Corporation. On this as on so many other socio-economic changes of the early eighteenth century, Defoe provides our most informative contemporary commentary. The widespread involvement of wealthy men in the stocks of the newer corporations, Defoe explains, is

one thing which makes such a constant daily intercourse between the Court part of the town, and the city; and this is given as one of the principal causes of the prodigious conflux of the nobility and gentry from all parts of England to London, more than ever was known in former years, viz. That many thousands of families are so deeply concerned in those stocks, and find it so absolutely necessary to be at hand to take the advantage of buying and selling, as the sudden rise or fall of the price directs. . . .

This is the reason why, notwithstanding the encrease of new buildings, and the addition of new cities, as they may be called, every year to the old, yet a house is no sooner built, but 'tis tenanted and inhabited, and every part is crouded with people, and that not only in the town, but in all the towns and villages round.[19]

So dependent was this expanded population on the new corporations, Defoe argues, that if a continuing peace should enable the government to pay off the public debt funded by the corporations, then the resultant slackening of stockjobbery would send many of the new London residents back to the country. Defoe therefore counsels moderation in continuing the building. The shrinking of London that he wrote of did not come; but, as I have said, the expansion all but stopped in the 1730's.

What were the consequences for the theaters of the economic changes and the consequent growth of London? They may be read in the changing location of theaters and in the changing composition of audiences.

In the years from the Restoration to 1705, the leading theaters—Drury Lane, Lincoln's Inn Fields, the Duke's, and Dorset Garden—were all east of Covent Garden, in "the middle Part of the Town." In the early years after the Restoration, when few citizens attended the theater, Drury Lane seems to have had the most advantageous location. Dryden, in an epilogue recited there in 1674, contrasts the favorable location of the theater with that of Dorset Garden, at the east end of Fleet Street:

> Our House relieves the Ladies from the frights
> Of ill pav'd Streets, and long dark Winter Nights;
> The *Flanders* Horses from a cold bleak Road,
> Where Bears in Furs dare scarcely look abroad.[20]

And Cibber, in the first years of the eighteenth century, accounting for the reverses of Betterton's company acting in Lincoln's Inn Fields, mentions the theater's "too distant Situation,"[21] meaning, apparently, from the residences of the gentry, for the other theater then operating was Drury Lane. Yet in the early eighteenth century the "citizens"—as distinguished from the gentry and the peerage—became an increasingly important part of the audience. In describing the adverse effect on Drury Lane of the opening of Lincoln's Inn Fields under John Rich in 1714, Cibber comments bitterly that he and his fellow managers knew Rich's company "would intercept many an honest Customer that might not know a good Market from a bad one."[22] Most patrons of the theaters, however, were in those years moving west. When John Rich moved his company in 1732 from Lincoln's Inn Fields to the new Covent Garden theater, he went westward of Drury Lane. Cibber is very informative on how the Haymarket's location increased in value from the time of its construction in 1705 until the time he wrote his Apology in 1738:

To this Inconvenience [of the playhouse] why may we not add that of its Situation; for at that time it had not the Advantage of almost a large City, which has since been built in its Neighbourhood: Those costly Spaces of *Hanover, Grosvenor,* and *Cavendish* Squares, with the many and great adjacent Streets about them, were then all but so many green Fields of Pasture, from whence they could draw little or no Sustenance, unless it were that of a Milk-Diet. The City, the Inns of Court, and the middle Part of the Town, which were the most constant Support of a Theatre, and chiefly to be relied on, were now too far out of the Reach of an easy Walk, and Coach-hire is often too hard a Tax upon the Pit and Gallery. But from the vast Increase of the Buildings I have mention'd, the Situation of that Theatre has since that Time received considerable Advantages; a new World of People of Condition are nearer to it than formerly.[23]

A conspicuous exception to the pattern of westward extension of theatrical activity was provided by the opening of a theater in Goodman's Fields, just over a mile *east* of St. Paul's Cathedral, in 1729. The theater, which was thus in East London, had some success, though it met opposition from the magistrates. A journalist, writing in *The Comedian, or Philosophical Enquirer*, No. 7 (October 1732), commented on the significance of the theater's location:

The Theatre next in Reputation to that of *Drury-lane* is that in *Goodman's-fields*; the Success of which, against the Opposition that has been made to it, discovers, in Part, the Spirit of Liberty now prevailing, and is likewise some Indication of Taste in a Part of the Town where Nothing but Avarice and other Sordidness were supposed to be.

Despite objection from magistrates and citizens, who feared that the working people living nearby would be debauched, the theater survived, with one minor change in location, until the time of Garrick. It evoked denunciatory pamphlets in a moralistic vein not unlike some antistage tracts which had appeared a century earlier.[24]

Apart from that of Goodman's Fields, the audience of the early-eighteenth-century theaters continued to be dominated by people of fashion. The audiences became larger—witness the statement of Dennis already quoted—but the percentage of those who pretended to fashion remained about the same. The important changes seem rather to have been in the components of the *beau monde* on the one hand and the citizenry on the other. Many of the merchants attending the theater, no longer considered "citizens," were accepted in the audience as gentlemen; many of the prominent financiers, performing functions that earlier were performed by citizens, belonged to gentle or even noble families. The citizens recognized as such in the early-eighteenth-century theater were not the leading members of the business community, the exporters and financiers, but rather the petty traders, the shopkeepers, and the apprentices. The social relationships of the audiences, then, remained constant on the surface; but the substance of the relationships, especially as they affected the business community, underwent an important change.

We have several descriptions of theatrical audiences at the end of the seventeeth and in the early eighteenth centuries, of which one of the most informative was published in 1698 by a French traveler to London:

> Il y a deux Théatres à Londres, l'un grand & beau, où se fait tantôt l'Opera, tantôt la Comédie: l'autre Théatre, qui est plus petit, n'est que pour la Comédie. Le Parterre est en Amphithéatre, & rempli de bancs sans dossiers; garnis & couverts d'une étofe verte. Les hommes de qualité, particulierement les jeunes gens; quelques Dames sages & honnêtes; & beaucoup de Filles qui cherchent fortune, s'asseyent tous là pelle mêle; causent, joüent, badinent, écoutent, n'écoutent pas. Plus loin, contre le mur, sous la premiere Galerie, & vis à vis de la Scene, s'éléve un autre Amphitheatre qui est occupé par les personnes de la plus haute Qualité, entre lesquelles on voit peu d'hommes. Les Galeries, dont il y a seulement un double rang, ne sont remplies que de gens du commun, particulierement celles d'en haut.[25]

We may supplement this description with a casual but informative allusion to the components of the audience made by George Farquhar in *A Discourse upon Comedy* in 1702. Farquhar describes the heterogeneous group whom a playwright must please: "Here is a pit full of Covent-Garden gentlemen, a gallery full of citts, a hundred ladies of court-education, and about two hundred footmen of nice morality."[26] Footmen sat in the upper gallery (without charge for admission);[27] "citizens" sat in the middle gallery; and people of fashion sat in the pit or the boxes, ladies as well as gentlemen of the highest rank usually sitting in the boxes. Since the purchasers of pit and box seats provided much the larger part of the theaters' receipts, the playwrights understandably tried to please them.

In an essay of 1702 Dennis, while explaining the causes of an alleged degeneracy in taste for drama, analyzes changes in the fashionable part of the audience since Charles II's time:

> There are three sorts of People now in our Audiences, who have had no education at all; and who were unheard of in the Reign of King *Charles* the Second. A great many younger Brothers, Gentlemen born, who have been kept at home, by reason of the pressure of the Taxes. Several People, who made their Fortunes in the late

War; and who from a state of obscurity, and perhaps of misery, have risen to a condition of distinction and plenty. I believe that no man will wonder, if these People, who in their original obscurity, could never attain to any higher entertainment than Tumbling and Vaulting and Ladder Dancing, and the delightful diversions of *Jack Pudding*, should still be in Love with their old sports, and encourage these noble Pastimes still upon the Stage. But a 3d sort of People, who may be said to have had no education at all in relation to us and our Plays, is that considerable number of Foreigners, which within these last twenty years have been introduc'd among us.[28]

I shall later consider Dennis's accusations against the theaters; at the moment, I confine myself to his remark about men who made their fortune in the course of the late war (the War of the League of Augsburg). Most of these men would have been merchants. At the time Dennis writes, the War of the Spanish Succession, which was to produce still more new fortunes for merchants, was just getting under way. Swift complained bitterly in the *Examiner* in 1710 and 1711 about the number of new men who had made fortunes as a result of that war; and that many of these men attended the theater we may assume from Charles Gildon's complaint in 1710 about the "Abundance of odd Spectators, whom the Chance of War have enabled to crowd the Pit and Stage-Boxes, and sway too much by their Thoughtless and Arbitrary Censure, either to the Advantage or Prejudice of the *Author* and *Player*."[29] Apparently, then, changes in those seated in the pit and the boxes constituted the most important differences between the early-eighteenth-century audience and that of the Restoration.

Dramatists seem to have been aware of the newcomers to the pit and the boxes, occasionally alluding to them in dramatic dialogue. "I wonder, the Play-house is not divided here as the Theatre at *Rome* us'd to be," observes a character in Thomas Baker's *The Humour of the Age* (1701), "where every one sat according to his respective Quality, and not as he was able to pay."[30] And a character in William Burnaby's *The Reformed Wife* (1700): "My great Diversion is to turn my Eyes upon the Middle Gallery;—or when a Citizen crowds her self in among us, 'tis an unspeakable Pleasure to contemplate her Airs and her Dress—And they never escape me; for I am as apprehensive of such Creatures coming near

me, as some People are when a Cat is in the Room—,"[31] a remark intended to provide an ironical reflection on the speaker,
but one which is informative nonetheless.

Sensitive to the pit and the boxes as the most remunerative
part of the audience, playwrights cared little for the footmen
in the upper gallery and perhaps not much more for the shopkeepers and artisans in the middle gallery. Certainly they continued to make derogatory allusions to "cits" in the audience
throughout the early part of the century, allusions which suggest that the term "citizen" was acquiring a more specialized
meaning than it had at the Restoration, when it was used even
with reference to a businessman operating on a more or less
large scale. Progressively in the early eighteenth century the
term was restricted to humble members of the mercantile community—partly because the more important members were
moving out of the City. The use of the term in the epilogue
of Susannah Centlivre's *The Platonic Lady* (1706) is informative:

> Some Cheapside-Bobbs too trudge it to our Play,
> Faith, Jack, this Hay-Market's a cursed Way:
> What signifie the Quality or Wits,
> The Money, Daniel, rises from us Cits.
> Who, like Cock-Sparrows, hop about the Benches,
> And court, with Six-pences, fat Orange-Wenches.

So also its use in the prologue of a revival of Fielding's *The
Author's Farce* (probably 1734):

> At seven now into our empty pit
> Drops from his counter some old prudent cit,
> Contented with twelve-pennyworth of wit.

As I shall point out later, playwrights came progressively to
distinguish between great merchants and citizens among their
dramatic characters.

The citizens did not go to plays in large numbers. The
theaters in early-eighteenth-century London never attracted
more than a minute fraction of the total population; certainly
they had no such popular audience as those of the Elizabethan
age had or that modern motion picture theaters have. A recent
comprehensive study of the theatrical audience in the middle
of the eighteenth century arrives at the interesting conclusion

that in the years of Garrick's management after 1750 only about 1.7 per cent of London's population attended the theater.[32] This figure will at least suggest the approximate size of attendance in the earlier part of the century. More theaters were operating (intermittently) before 1737 than after 1750, but the earlier theaters were not so large. (Only two theaters operated consistently in both periods.) The price of admission was very high in relation to the wages of working people— much higher than in Elizabethan times—so that few of them could afford to attend the theater even if they were interested in doing so or had the time after their long hours of work.

❧ TWO ❧

Social Rivalry and Critical Controversy

The redistribution of families that accompanied the growth of London produced social tensions by placing together as neighbors persons of sharply different social backgrounds, at a time when egalitarian ideas had as yet gained little acceptance. Of these tensions the drama gives us a record, though not one that can be read uncritically.

The opposition between the mercantile City and the fashionable west end had provided comedies with themes for a long time before the eighteenth century—indeed, before the theaters were closed by the Puritans. For example, Massinger's *City Madam* (1632), which ridicules the affectations of the socially ambitious Lady Frugal and ends with her accepting her lot as an unfashionable merchant's wife. Still, Lady Frugal did remain in the City, even at the height of her folly. Caroline and Restoration drama exhibit many foolish, vain, and ambitious City wives (some of them, of course, game for fashionable gallants) as well as doting and miserly City husbands. Yet these characters, numerous as they are, never receive understanding, sympathetic treatment; the sympathy of the dramatists—Massinger, Jonson, Shirley, Wycherley, and Congreve —was so overwhelmingly on the side of the fashionable that their citizens remained little more than stupid, immoral fools— Alderman Fondlewives and Alderman Gripes. The dramatists wanted the spectators to identify themselves with the fashionable and to regard the citizens as outlanders for whom no imaginative sympathy was required.

There was, not a sharp change, but a perceptible modification of social values in comedy roughly coincident with the turn of the century. This modification was accelerated by the dramatic reform movement and by the related rejection in drama of the medieval economic theory which had deeply colored Jonson's and Massinger's social philosophy.

The comedies of Jonson, Middleton, Massinger, and other Elizabethan and Jacobean dramatists clearly reveal the dramatists' hostility to the acquisitiveness of the mercantile society then just coming into being.[1] The pervasive theme of Jonson's comedies is the evil of an inordinate lust for wealth. The dramatists were equally hard on social ambition; Shakespeare, for example, was unmerciful in dealing with Malvolio's efforts to improve himself. "The England of Shakespeare and Bacon was still largely mediaeval in its economic organization and social outlook," writes Professor Tawney,

more interested in maintaining customary standards of consumption than in accumulating capital for future production, with an aristocracy contemptuous of the economic virtues, a peasantry farming for subsistence amid the organized confusion of the open-field village, and a small, if growing, body of jealously conservative craftsmen.[2]

But all of this changed in the course of the seventeenth century as England turned increasingly to the doctrines of mercantilism. Economic individualism came not merely to be tolerated but to be encouraged as the mainspring of an expanding economy. The great entrepreneur became too valuable to the nation and too powerful to be despised. The dramatists were slow in acknowledging the change; but by the early eighteenth century they were compelled to acknowledge it.

Although it is not uncommon for writers of imaginative literature to be in the forefront of social thinking, precisely the reverse was true of the dramatists of the seventeenth century; they gave expression to social ideas and attitudes only after they had long been accepted by large portions of the nation. The reason for this conservatism is not far to seek: throughout most of the century the drama was supported by the landed classes, who were conservative, and was opposed—at times even suppressed—by the mercantile classes, who were liberal in at least some aspects of economic thought. The drama gives a thoroughly inadequate impression of the seventeenth-century merchant, and of the mercantile life in which he was central. Even by the end of the sixteenth century, London was a highly developed financial center, with an important commercial class;[3] but the dramatists, without significant exception, treated commerce, if at all, in economic and ethical categories of social responsibility appropriate to a precommercial age. The memorable business figures—Sir Giles Overreach in *A New Way to Pay Old Debts*, for example, and the Citizen in *The Knight of the Burning Pestle*—are satirical characters. Where mercantile life is sympathetically presented, it is likely to be treated in the nostalgic terms of *The Shoemaker's Holiday*, with its setting in the fifteenth century. As long as the Elizabethan dramatists applied the traditional criteria of social obligations to mercantile life, they found it censurable, for it was outgrowing the bounds within which the old standards were relevant. The government supported efforts to make prevail the older theory of society as a hierarchy in which each had his established place and duties,[4] and the dramatists accepted the official theory—until the civil war intervened.

The war accelerated the adjustment of economic theory to economic fact: it put an end to the government's attempt to hold society in the molds inherited from the time before commercial expansion, and it saw an effective government effort to improve trade. Even at the Restoration, attended as it was by many repressive measures, there was no widespread inclination to return to an economic theory based on the mutual obligations of classes; on the contrary, there was a growing inclination, stimulated by the scientific movement and the political arithmeticians, to consider economic forces impersonally, without regard to ethical and religious positions. Some individual thinkers, notably Bunyan and Baxter, continued to apply religious criteria to economic relations in the old way; but after the Restoration theirs was distinctly a minority attitude.

Though the official socio-economic attitudes of the Restoration were better disposed to mercantile activity than those of the reigns of Elizabeth and the earlier Stuarts, the merchant was treated even more bitterly in Restoration comedy than he was in the earlier comedy. The predominantly Nonconformist mercantile community, after all, had supported attacks on the stage since Elizabethan times and had supported the government that closed the theaters during the interregnum. The intensely royalist courtiers who composed the theatrical audience of the early years after the Restoration remembered the London financiers' support of Cromwell. As the resentments

engendered by the civil war cooled, dramatic tradition perpetuated the plots and character types fixed when the mid-century
battles were a burning memory. Thus, Congreve, born ten
years after the Restoration, includes in *The Old Bachelor*
(1693) a character, Alderman Fondlewife, who resembles in
essentials a character in Wycherley's much earlier *Love in a
Wood* (1671), "Alderman *Gripe*, seemingly precise, but a
covetous, leacherous, old Usurer of the City," a bitter caricature of a London financier who is a hypocritical Puritan and
was formerly a supporter of Cromwell.

Wycherley may have written a first draft of *Love in a
Wood* as early as 1659-60, at the end of the Commonwealth
period;[5] but whether then or later, he wrote the play in the grip
of antipathies deriving from the interregnum. "You have
broken many an Oath for the good old cause" (V), a character
remarks to Alderman Gripe; and another character describes
him as "a prying Common-Wealths-man, an implacable Majes-
trate, a sturdy pillar of his cause" (I). In conversation, Gripe
employs the usages of Puritanism, which have a comic incongruity in his lecherous schemes. Gripe is a "scrivener," grown
rich in moneylending—an activity subjected to satire. One
character refers to him contemptuously as a "Jew" (V), because of his occupation, not his race. Gripe, who thus is a com-
posite of the religious, political, and personal qualities that
were odious to Wycherley and his patrons at court, is in the
course of the dramatic action deprived of his daughter, de-
frauded of his money, and exposed in a futile attempt at lech-
ery. Neither in this play nor in his others does Wycherley
depart from such partisan views of businessmen.

Congreve, unlike Wycherley, had no personal knowledge
of the Commonwealth, but his judgments are essentially Wycherley's. Fondlewife, a rich banker and foreign trader, is a pious
and hypocritical Nonconformist, a member of a despised class
who is a fair target for the insouciant young gentlemen. Bellmour, one of the gentlemen, gains access to Laetitia, Fondlewife's young wife, by disguising himself in the garb of Spin-
text, a Nonconformist clergyman friend and spiritual adviser
of Fondlewife. Even in this play, then, written in the 1690's,
the social judgments implicit in the satire resemble those of a
Royalist during the civil war. Fondlewife, an eminent "mer-

chant and trader by sea," in the contemporary phrase, is damned as an avaricious, uxorious, canting hypocrite.

It was against this background of deep social conservatism that an extended critical review of the theater was carried on from about 1695 to about 1745. There was general agreement that the theater deserved severe criticism on various grounds. The criticism assumed two main patterns: one was moralistic, the criticism of Jeremy Collier and his allies, who as a group were sympathetic to the business community; the other was aesthetic, the criticism of Pope in the *Dunciad* and of the many writers in agreement with him on artistic principles, who were largely hostile to the business community and what it represented. Some writers, of course, combined moralistic and aesthetic criticism: nearly all of the dramatists and critics who replied to Collier acknowledged that some plays were reprehensibly licentious; and nearly all of the reformers, including Collier himself, employed arguments derived from critical theory. Yet in nearly every instance it is possible to determine whether a given piece of theatrical criticism is dominated by moralistic or aesthetic considerations: whether, that is, the critic had more in common with Jeremy Collier in *A Short View of the Immorality and Profaneness of the English Stage* or with Pope in the *Dunciad*. Needless to say, the critical attitudes had social correlatives that influenced the drama.

From the earliest times to the present, there has been a strong element of continuity in attacks on the stage—so strong, in fact, as to suggest that such attacks derive from some deep and recurring qualities of the human personality. In England critics of the stage have had a traditionalist bent: they have habitually cited earlier critics of the stage, even to the extent of drawing from common sources among the early Christian and classical writers. It has indeed been shown that scarcely any new grounds for criticism of the stage appeared after the sixth century.[6] Thus it is that the attacks of Stephen Gosson in 1579, of William Prynne in 1632, and of Collier in 1698 have a strong common element.

The similarities between Prynne's attack and Collier's are,

to be sure, obscured by a marked difference in the religious and political positions of the two men: Prynne was a Puritan and an enemy of the Stuarts, whereas Collier was a high church Anglican, so devoted to the Stuarts that he refused to take the oaths of allegiance to King William. Prynne was a spokesman of the Puritan movement, which had long opposed the stage; Collier gave allegiance to a King who had patronized the stage and to a church that had been sympathetic to it. Nonetheless, there was historical continuity between the social groups for which they were spokesmen, and contemporaries of Collier associated his attack with that of Prynne and of the Puritans. Collier was moved to attack the stage, not by social or political considerations, but by the deep religious conviction that the stage was conducive to sin. His primary motive for writing *A Short View* was religious, just as Prynne's was in writing *Histriomastix*. Because religious issues were entangled with social and even economic ones, however, both Prynne's and Collier's books had wider implications, and implications of a similar nature.

From the time the theaters were reopened in 1660 until just a few years before *A Short View* in 1698, there was almost no open opposition to the stage. The reason is clear enough: a public attack on the stage would have been politically dangerous. For one thing, theater haters had killed Charles I; moreover, both Charles II and James II were active patrons of the theater. Yet enough evidence of grumblings about the stage during these reigns has been preserved for us to know that, though the opposition may have been inarticulate, it nevertheless existed.[7]

William III's political position and his indifference to the stage made it possible for critics to speak out. When in the 1690's they did so, many observers saw in their complaints a renewal of the earlier Puritan complaints. Dryden's reply to Sir Richard Blackmore, who wrote the most important of the pre-Collier attacks in the 1690's, associates Blackmore with the "fanatics": "As for the City Bard, or Knight Physician," Dryden wrote in the preface to the *Fables* (1700), "I hear his quarrel to me is, that I was the author of 'Absalom and Achitophel,' which, he thinks, is a little hard on his fanatic patrons in London."[8] In their replies to *A Short View*, a number of critics and dramatists (among them Congreve, Dennis, Thomas Baker, Cibber, Tom Brown, and Elkanah Settle) associated Collier with the mid-century Puritans.

"I presume I need not tell the World," wrote Defoe in the *Review*, May 25, 1710, "that the Principal Body of the *Dissenters*, in *England*, lies among the Trading People of the Nation; Merchandizing and Manufacturing, is generally speaking their Province." Later in the same essay, Defoe estimates that the Dissenters comprise at least one-half of "the Trading, Merchandizing, Manufacturing, and Shop-keeping part of *England*." Other contemporary observers, including Voltaire, commented on the disproportionate number of Dissenters who were prominent in industry and finance.[9] Many of the leaders in mercantile life were Anglicans, and a few even were Catholics; but the Dissenters, in various casts of religious opinion, formed a very influential portion of the business community. Since the Dissenters of London were the inheritors of the Puritan tradition, the alliance of merchant and Dissent has important implications for the relations of the theater with the business community.

Jeremy Collier was a churchman and a zealot above all, and had he been inclined to enter social controversies, he would scarcely have supported the dissenting merchants. His *Short View*, in fact, expresses a strong social conservatism. But because it articulated grievances that the merchants had long felt against the gentry and nobility, the controversy it initiated took the form of class antagonism.

The dramatists assumed, in their replies to the reformers, an alliance between the reformers and the mercantile City,

> Where a Prim Face, and Holy Affectation,
> Palm Cheating on the Town for Reformation,

in the words of a prologue writer of 1713.[10] Plays produced in the wake of the stage controversy contain many satirical allusions, embedded in dialogue, to the association of City and reform. Thus Sir Thrifty Gripe, a merchant in William Burnaby's *The Ladies' Visiting Day* (1701), associates his own sharp practices in trade with his reforming zeal (I): "I live soberly, and mind the main Chance, I never spend a Penny but in Coffee; I sell by a short Yard, and pull down the Play Bills, to shew my Aversion to the Wickedness that's practis'd there." Deputy Driver, in Thomas Baker's *An Act at Oxford* (1704), a "Stockjobber, City Reformer, and chief Beggar-Hunter," speaks similarly of himself (I): "Why, Friend, I'm one that will have thee turn'd out o' Commission for a Debauch'd Magistrate, and put into the Black List for a Promoter of Gluttony, and Drunkenness, in Opposition to *frugal Sobriety*, and the Reform'd City of *London*."

The most bitter dramatic attack on the merchant reformers appears in George Farquhar's *The Constant Couple* (1699). The contempt for the merchants here revealed, much more severe than that exhibited in any of Farquhar's other plays, was intensified, I suspect, by Farquhar's resentment of the merchants' part in the reform movement that had erupted the year before with *A Short View*. Farquhar makes a special point of the association of Alderman Smuggler, an utterly despicable character, with the stage reformers. Smuggler tells Lady Lurewell of his reputation as a reformer while attempting to seduce her (II); and again in another episode, in a conversation with a young apprentice turned beau, he denounces the stage (V):

Ay, you must go to the Plays too, Sirrah: Lord, Lord! What Business has a Prentice at a Play-house, unless it be to hear his Master made a Cuckold, and his Mistriss a Whore? 'Tis ten to one now, but some malicious Poet has my Character upon the Stage within this Month: 'Tis a hard matter now, that an honest sober Man can't sin in private for this plaguy Stage. I gave an honest Gentleman five Guineas my self towards writing a Book against it: And it has done no good, we see.

Smuggler's "honest Gentleman" would have been identified as Jeremy Collier.

The dramatic reform movement, then, was but a striking episode in a controversy about the stage that had gone on for generations and that had long been associated with an antagonism between social classes. But as it developed at the end of the seventeenth century, it became entangled with new issues, at the same time literary and social, that were not confined to the drama. In its contemporary context the dramatic reform movement must also be considered as part of a more inclusive controversy about the proper function of "wit" in literature.

The dramatists of the later seventeenth century, who were the chief objects of Collier's criticism, were wits in one of the contemporary meanings of that ubiquitous term; and they were in their plays practitioners of witty writing. Now for reasons associated with the deepest intellectual currents of the age, wit was under attack in the late seventeenth and early eighteenth centuries.[11]

There were indeed many who regarded wit (considered as an aspect of the creative faculty), as in practice, if not necessarily in theory, a downright evil. They characteristically based their opinion not on philosophical arguments but rather on the demonstrably impious uses served by much of the literature, dramatic and nondramatic, on which wit had been expended. As in the assault on the stage, so in the assault on wit, some of the strongest critics were puritanical Nonconformists who had associations with the business community.

The literary career of Sir Richard Blackmore, more than that of any other man, brought to a review the conflicting attitudes toward wit—not so much those based on reasoned philosophical positions as those based on social, economic, and religious positions.[12] His most comprehensive discussion of wit came late in his career, in his *Essay upon Wit* (1716). Not hostile to the existence of imaginative literature (as a practicing poet he could scarcely be), he nevertheless exhibits a utilitarian disposition of mind incompatible with a high regard for it:

The Labours of the meanest Persons, that conduce to the Welfare and Benefit of the Publick, are more valuable, because more useful, than the Employments of those, who apply themselves only, or principally, to divert and entertain the Fancy; and therefore must be as much preferable to the Occupation or Profession of a Wit, as the Improvement and Happiness of Men is to be regarded above their Mirth and Recreation.[13]

Tolerant at best of literature not immediately didactic, Blackmore was critical in this essay, as throughout his career, of contemporary poets and dramatists; and his criticism turned on their alleged abuse of wit. He offers a definition of the term in this essay: *"Wit is a Qualification of the Mind, that raises and enlivens cold Sentiments and plain Propositions, by giving them an elegant and surprizing Turn.*"[14] In short, he considered wit, as did Locke and many others, to be primarily ornamental.

Blackmore began his campaign against the abuse of wit—and against "the wits"—in 1695, in the Preface to the first of his ponderous and inept epics, *Prince Arthur*. Three years before *A Short View* he denounces the stage, if less forcefully and specifically than Collier, still in many of the same particulars. Blackmore's remarks on the abuse of wit in drama form but an extended interpolation in this Preface directed to the epic. The purpose of literature, he insists, is the inculcation of religious and ethical principles. "They are Men of little Genius," he writes, "of mean and poor Design, that imploy their Wit for no higher Purpose than to please the Imagination of vain and wanton People."[15] Most of the practicing playwrights and some of the nondramatic poets, he maintains, far from being merely useless, are destructive of the morality and religion of those who read or hear their productions. "The sweetness of the Wit makes the *Poison* go down with Pleasure, and the Contagion spreads without Opposition."[16] In a passage that Collier and Steele later echo, he describes the leading character in comedy:

The *Man of Sense*, and the *Fine* Gentleman in the *Comedy*, who, as the chiefest Person propos'd to the Esteem and Imitation of the Audience, is enrich'd with all the Sense and Wit the Poet can bestow—this *Extraordinary Person* you will find to be a *Derider* of Religion, a great *Admirer* of *Lucretius*, not so much for his *Learning* as his *Irreligion*, a Person wholly *Idle*, dissolv'd in Luxury, abandon'd to his Pleasures, a great Debaucher of Women, profuse and extravagant in his Expences; and, in short, this *Finish'd Gentleman* will appear a *Finish'd Libertine.*[17]

When Blackmore calls this character a "Gentleman," he uses the word in its specialized sense; and in fact he expresses a well-defined merchant-class bias in his denunciation of the dramatic stereotypes of the citizen and the alderman, as well as in his objection to the dramatic cuckolding of citizens: "In our *Comedies* the *Wives of Citizens* are highly encourag'd to despise their Husbands, and to make great Friendship with some such *Vertuous Gentleman* and *Man of Sense* as is above describ'd."[18]

In the Preface to his *King Arthur* (1697) Blackmore renews his criticism of alleged literary and dramatic abuses; and this time he attributes the criticism of *Prince Arthur* to the fact that he is not one of the group of writers who surround Dryden in Covent Garden.[19] In 1699, in his *Satire against Wit,* he becomes quite personal in abuse of Dryden and literary men in his circle. He describes the pernicious effects of wit:

> Wit does enfeeble and debauch the Mind,
> Before to Business or to Arts inclin'd.
> How useless is a Sauntering empty Wit,
> Only to please with Jests at Dinner fit?[20]

This is oversimplified literary criticism, motivated by private pique, expressing a sectarian bias. The wits resented the poem, as they had resented Blackmore's earlier criticism; and they found in Blackmore, who had a naïve opinion of the merit of his epics, an easy target for ridicule.

The result was *Commendatory Verses, on the Author of the Two Arthurs, and the Satire against Wit* (March 1700), a collection of lampoons, most of them written by Dryden's circle, collected and edited, apparently, by Tom Brown. In this volume, and in the retaliatory volume which appeared the following month, *Discommendatory Verses, on Those Which are Truly Commendatory, on the Author of the Two Arthurs, and the Satire against Wit,* the association of Blackmore with the City and the wits with fashionable Covent Garden is freely acknowledged. It is the full understanding and acknowledgment, on both sides, of the social alignment that gives this exchange of lampoons, most of them petty improvisations, some minor significance in literary history.[21] Coming as it did only two years after Collier's *Short View,* and before the flurry of pamphleteering occasioned by that tract had subsided, Blackmore's quarrel with the wits was inevitably associated with the stage dispute. Both Collier and Blackmore were moralistic critics of the stage who drew strong support from the merchant class; both were considered by hostile contemporaries to be writing in the tradition of the mid-seventeenth-century Puritans; and both were humorless men whose literary sensitivity was blunted by religious zeal. A popular lampoon suggests their mutual hostility to Dryden, until his death in 1700 the acknowledged leader of the wits:

> John Dryden enemies had three,
> Sir Dick, Old Nick, and Jeremy:
> The doughty knight was forced to yield,
> The other two have kept the field.[22]

Leaving the devil out of account, Collier of the remaining two certainly was the more effective in controversy; and he probably had the deeper influence. But it is not fair to say that Blackmore lost his bout with the wits.

Throughout his career he attracted favorable comment from the like-minded, from Samuel Wesley and Daniel Defoe, for example. Wesley, an Anglican, though one of a puritanical disposition who had been educated as a Dissenter, published in 1700 *An Epistle to a Friend Concerning Poetry*, a verse treatise in the manner of Pope's *Essay on Criticism* of a decade later. Although mainly concerned with critical problems, Wesley endorses both Collier and Blackmore in their respective controversies; interestingly enough, moreover, he associates his own endeavor with that of Prynne.[23] Defoe's poem *The Pacificator* (1700), an account of a fictional war between two contending groups of authors, sides with the men of sense though not without an interesting metaphorical reservation.

> *Wit* is a King without a Parliament,
> And *Sense* a Democratick Government.[24]

Gradually, Blackmore attracted support from among those who earlier were critical of him, notably from Steele and Addison. If not unqualified, the support was consistent with accomplishing the ends that Blackmore had proposed, and it was immensely influential. The *Tatler* and the *Spectator* can be considered to have resolved the differences between Blackmore and the wits, in so far as the differences were ones of principle and not merely personal. A purpose of the periodicals, their authors boasted, was to bring wit to the service of morality; and this purpose was realized, according to John Gay, among others.[25] The *Tatler* and the *Spectator* are didactic with determination, and they attack most of the faults that Blackmore—and Collier—had denounced; but they employ the sprightliness, the humor, and the learning that the wits had exhibited. The essays include discussions of wit—of true wit, of false wit, of misdirected wit—and they offer an example of wit responsibly used. In social attitudes, too, they show an assimilation of the best of what in the quarrel of 1700 were antithetical positions. In Mr. Spectator's club, merchant and gentleman meet on terms of cordiality. If in the essays there is a perceptible bias in favor of the merchants (certainly there is not a strong one), it is arguable that such a bias was needed to correct the balance of contemporary opinion.

Collier, Blackmore, Defoe, Addison, and Steele, to take the most prominent figures on the side of the reformers, were alike in protesting "the immorality and profaneness" of the stage. But they differed among each other sharply: Collier, Blackmore, and Defoe opposed the existence of the stage as, in their belief, conducive to sin; and Addison and Steele, both of them playwrights and dramatic critics, supported the stage as potentially beneficial. The gulf between these two groups, and between their followers, was wide and relations were not always cordial. Blackmore criticized Addison in the *Satyr against Wit*; Steele was among the wits who ridiculed Blackmore in *Commendatory Verses*; Defoe attacked Steele in a pamphlet of 1715 for encouraging theater attendance.[26] On the other hand, Addison and Steele and Blackmore came to have a cordial regard for each other: Addison, in fact, praised Blackmore's *Creation* in the *Spectator*.[27] Steele, in his *Apology*, acknowledged himself a follower of Collier.[28]

Nonetheless, the five men would scarcely have thought of themselves as engaged in a common cause. On the contrary, Addison and Steele—especially Steele—were forced by the more extreme reformers to take up the task of defending the stage's right to exist. Steele's many essays praising actors, plays, and the theater as an institution can be fully understood only in the context of the puritanical opposition he faced from such men as Collier, Blackmore, Defoe, and, a little later, William Law. Steele employed his persuasive gifts in the *Tatler*, the *Spectator*, the *Guardian*, the *Town Talk*, and the *Theatre* to convince his readers, many of whom belonged to social groups that had only recently begun to take an interest in literature, that the theater, in so far as it was not morally offensive, deserved support. Committed politically to the merchants, Steele tried in his essays and by the example of *The Conscious Lovers* to make the theater more hospitable to them.

Steele and Addison were of course far from alone in the propagandistic effort in support of the theater. The continuing effort is well illustrated by two anonymous essays that appeared in *The British Journal, Or the Traveller*, as late as December 5 and December 26, 1730, respectively, prompted by the citizens' protests against the opening of Goodman's Fields Theatre in East London. The writer undertakes, somewhat naïvely, a critical examination, first of *King Lear* and later of *The Squire of Alsatia*, giving attention to "the Moral Part" in order to demonstrate "the Advantages which arise to a Nation from the Encouragement of Arts." "Where can Youth more properly go," he asks, "than where they are not only taught but have presented to their Eyes, what are the Rewards of Virtue, and what the woeful Fruits of Vice?" His question suggests that the way was prepared for Lillo's *The London Merchant; Or, The History of George Barnwell* of the following year.

We are likely, in retrospect, to underestimate the seriousness of the threat posed by the reformers to the survival of the theaters. Because the reformers did not succeed in closing them, we may forget that in 1698, when men could still remember the interregnum, the issue of the Collier controversy seemed to many observers to be in doubt. Such an essay as Dennis's *The Usefulness of the Stage* (1698) is informative in its assumption that the audience of reasonable men to whom it is addressed requires an extended demonstration of the social function of the drama. Although Dennis was partisan, he was not, in this essay, indulging his prejudices; rather, he was attempting with logical argument to help the theaters survive by winning the minds of the large body of men who were interested in the controversy. The theaters could no longer depend for their support and protection on a court faction; they must henceforth have popular support, and perforce support from the mercantile community, if they were to escape repressive legislation and were to attract profitable audiences.

A subsidiary aim of the dramatic reform movement was to accomplish a modification in the dramatic treatment of the merchant. The chief leaders of the movement, with the single exception of Collier, had active ties, either personal or political, with the merchant class. Blackmore's and Defoe's are apparent. Although Steele and Addison were gentlemen by birth, educated at Oxford, and in time landowners, they were active Whigs; and when such issues as the Landed Property Qualification Bill of 1711 and the commercial clauses of the Treaty of Utrecht brought to focus the opposition between merchants and landowners, they supported the merchants.

Blackmore includes a complaint about the merchant stereotype in the Preface to *Prince Arthur*: "To deter Men from being *Industrious* and *Wealthy*, the *Diligent*, *Thriving* Citizen is made the most Wretched, Contemptible Thing in the World."[29] Collier makes the same point with vehemence in *A Short View*,[30] though he objects also to the disrespectful dramatic treatment of the nobility. Steele, the most effective popularizer of Collier's precepts, asserted the dignity of the merchants throughout his career and included in *The Conscious Lovers* satirical hits at the gentry's disdain for them. In the *Spectator*, in Addison's papers as well as Steele's, appear complaints about the wits' treatment of the business community. Advising Mr. Spectator, Sir Andrew Freeport remarks (No. 34; by Addison): "In short, . . . if you avoid that foolish beaten Road of falling upon Aldermen and Citizens, and employ your Pen upon the Vanity and Luxury of Courts, Your Paper must needs be of general Use." Nor is this advice to be discounted as that of the fictional Sir Andrew. "If an Alderman appears upon the Stage," Addison observes in the same vein in a later essay (No. 446), "you may be sure it is in order to be Cuckolded."

The merchants' case against the dramatists is effectively summarized by an anonymous contributor to the *Universal Journal*, July 4, 1724:

> But of all the Characters generally drawn in our modern Comedies, we find none more falsly represented than that of the Citizens. People that know nothing more of 'em than what they see in Plays, think that of Course an Alderman must be an old, lecherous, griping Userer, or a doting Cuckold. Tell such as these of a generous and honest Citizen, they'll laugh at you, and look upon you as an ignorant Fellow, that knows nothing of the World; or be

affronted with you, thinking you intend to impose upon them by giving 'em an Account of People who never had a Being.

I do believe that there have been, and may be still, some few Citts of that Character; Perhaps some former Poet personally knew such a one, and had a Mind to expose him for differing so much from his Fellow Citizens; but how every Modern came to copy after him in this Particular, is somewhat strange. Even our two greatest Writers, *Congreve* and *Farquhar*, are fallen into the same customary Error. But throughout the whole Course of my Reading, I do not remember in any one of our Comedies to have seen a polite Citizen; and yet I am sure it is not for want of a sufficient Number of real Examples from which they might draw their Characters. I have before now known a Merchant fit to preside at the Board of Trade, and a Banker every way qualified for a Lord Treasurer.

View the Assemblies of our Citizens, when met on Business; attend a General Court, and you shall hear 'em debate with the same East, and the same Eloquence as at the Bar, or in the Senate: In Company with the Ladies we find 'em complaisant Gallants; they can there lay aside all Thoughts of Business, and enter on a Tea Table Topick with as much Humour as the best Lady's Man about Town.

The state of affairs described here is substantially the true one. The literary tradition responsible for the characterization of the merchant had lost contact with reality; citizen cuckolds in comedy begot their like. Years before this essay appeared in 1724, dramatists and critics had begun the task of restoring truth to comedy in this major area of social relations; but it was to be several years yet before the task was completed. The older comedies—of Wycherley, Congreve, and Farquhar—remained as staples of the theaters' repertories and thus helped to perpetuate the stereotypes.

In addition to the moralistic criticism of the drama, there was, as noted, a large body of aesthetic criticism—of which Pope's *Dunciad* is a preeminent example. The *Dunciad* is a summary statement of a theme that had wide currency in the early eighteenth century: the contemporary vulgarization of literature, dramatic as well as nondramatic, and especially the kind of vulgarization caused by the increasing size of the audience for literature. The action of the *Dunciad* is the progress of Dullness, a symbol in the poem of mercantile attitudes and

values, from the City to the court end of London:[31] the extension, that is, of the merchants' alleged intellectual and artistic
mediocrity to the court as well as to the thinking part of the
rest of the nation.

Pope gave special place to the theaters in the *Dunciad*, in
all versions satirizing the theatrical managers and in the final
version making Cibber, then poet laureate, his king. His poem
has close affinities with theatrical literature. He seems to have
taken suggestions for the fourth book of the *Dunciad* from
several of Fielding's burlesques of the 1730's.[32] And ante-
dating even the first version of Pope's poem, there is a considerable dunciad literature of the theater—burlesque writings
for and about the theater on the same general theme of vulgarization. Dryden's *Mac Flecknoe*, which in both theme and
satirical method anticipates the *Dunciad*, is in part a theatrical
poem. Pope's own *Peri Bathous* (1728), closely related thematically to the *Dunciad*, includes as its final chapter a burlesque "Project for the Advancement of the Stage." Indeed,
the alleged degeneracy of the stage was for years a popular
subject for criticism and satire, giving rise to extended works
as well as to brief satirical passages interpolated in essays, prefaces, dedications, prologues, and epilogues.

Of the denunciatory critics of the stage with an aesthetic
bias, John Dennis was easily the most articulate. From his
*A Large Account of the Taste in Poetry, and The Causes of
the Degeneracy of It* (1702) until his *The Causes of the Decay
and Defects of Dramatic Poetry, and of the Degeneracy of
the Public Taste* (about 1725), he lamented the condition of
the stage,[33] frequently comparing it unfavorably with that of
earlier times. His *Large Account* offers, among other things,
a detailed comparison between the taste for comedy in the reign
of Charles II, when it was "extremely good," and in the time
he is writing, when it is "excessively bad." What changes in
the intervening years, Dennis inquires, have produced the decline? The qualities necessary for appreciating good comedy,
as well as for writing it, he argues, are "1. Great parts. 2. A
generous Education. 3. A due Application."[34] Innate human
abilities in any age may be presumed to be equal, but historical
changes condition the effective development of them. "Now

I leave to any one to judge," he asks, "whether the imaginative faculty of the Soul, must be more exercised in a Reign of Poetry and of Pleasure, or in a Reign of Politicks and of Business."[35] Indeed, Dennis attributes the decline in taste in part to the contemporary preoccupation with politics and business, with which he associates a change in the composition of the audience.[36] Some of the new members of the audience, he argues,

have been Instrumental in introducing Sound and Show, where the business of the Theatre does not require it, and particularly a sort of a soft and wanton Musick, which has used the People to a delight which is independant of Reason, a delight that has gone a very great way towards the enervating and dissolving their minds.[37]

The terms of his criticism, it will be noted, resemble Pope's terms in the *Dunciad*. Whatever the personal differences between Dennis and Pope, their assessments of the literary taste of their contemporaries were similar.

Several nondramatic satires are devoted to the theaters, notably *The Battle of the Authors Lately Fought in Covent-Garden, Between Sir John Edgar, Generalissimo on One Side, and Horatius Truewit, on the Other* (1720), a mock-heroic prose narrative that structurally and thematically anticipates the *Dunciad*.[38] Written, according to its author (if we interpret aright his irony), "in Defence of Art and Knowledge, against Ignorance and the gay and modish Writings of the Times,"[39] the satire, having special reference to the theater, is an allegorical account of a battle in which the forces of Queen Ignorance contend unsuccessfully with the forces of Truewit. The allegory owes something to Swift's *Battle of the Books* and to Addison's *Spectator*, No. 63; and like the allegory in those works and in the *Dunciad* later it comprehends major issues from the recent controversy of the Ancients and Moderns. The affairs of Sir Richard Steele at Drury Lane provide a starting point for the satire, but the satire is generalized in a review of the contemporary literary scene which even in its bias is informative.

There are two opposing sides in *The Battle of the Authors*: the neoclassicists (Rymer, Dennis, and by implication the author himself) and those who scorn neoclassical precepts (Steele, Defoe, and Cibber). The former follow Truewit, the latter Queen Ignorance; the former support the Ancients, the latter the Moderns; and, although this is not explicit in the pamphlet, the former are clearly the literary champions of the nobility and gentry, the latter of the merchants. Steele's and Defoe's espousal of the merchants requires no elucidation. Cibber was not a propogandist for the merchants, yet his name was already a symbol for the managerial effort to satisfy the undisciplined popular taste; and in fact it was soon to become a symbol with opposition writers, of whom Pope was one, for the artistic degeneracy of Walpole's England.

Steele, Defoe, and Cibber all were writers who had experienced much popular success: Defoe in *Robinson Crusoe*, published just the year before *The Battle of the Authors*; Steele in his periodicals and in the management of Drury Lane. All three had caught public favor with work which bore little relation to neoclassicism: Steele and Cibber, in fact, advocated the violation of the neoclassical doctrine of kinds in comedy. Both of them had previously introduced pathetic incident into comedy, and Steele was known to be preparing the way, through critical writings, for a comedy (*The Conscious Lovers*) which would include exemplary characters. Further, Defoe and Steele were among the stage reformers; and Cibber, though he had initially been critical of Collier, was a leader in the experiments in writing "reformed" comedy. Of the writers active in 1720, these three—in the allegory the leaders of the army of Queen Ignorance—represent most clearly the trends in literature that can be associated with the literary enfranchisement of the merchant class.

A number of early-eighteenth-century plays are in intent more or less serious critiques of the stage, among which are *The What D'Ye Call It, Three Hours After Marriage, The Beggar's Opera, The Author's Farce, Tom Thumb, Pasquin,* and *Chrononhotonthologos.* The drama shared with nondramatic literature the early-eighteenth-century disposition toward satire; and much of the dramatic satire was directed at the stage itself. It has to do above all with the absurdities of sentiment and spectacle allegedly presented by the theatrical managers because they attracted remunerative audiences. There are strong elements of repetition and continuity in these plays, not so much because they were interdependent as because they were influenced by a common original—Buckingham's *The Rehearsal*, which in many adaptations had a prominent place in the early-eighteenth-century repertory.⁴⁰ The writers of these plays shared with Pope a fear that the age was one of cultural decline, and they adopted literary stratagems of protest that resemble his.

A brief farce somewhat resembling *The Battle of the Authors* was interpolated into a performance of *Tom Thumb* at the little theater in the Haymarket in November 1730, only a few days after it became known that Cibber had been chosen poet laureate.⁴¹ This farce, "The Battle of the Poets; Or, The Contention for the Laurel" by "Scriblerus Tertius" (probably a pseudonym of Thomas Cooke), was later printed with a quotation from the *Dunciad* on the title page, which in the context of Cibber's recent appointment—the subject of the burlesque—can be read as an advancement of the actor to the sovereignty of dullness some thirteen years before the appearance of the revised *Dunciad*:

> Now, Bavius, take the Poppy from thy Brow,
> And place it here! here all ye Heroes bow!
> This, this is He, foretold by ancient Rhimes,
> Th'Augustus born to bring Saturnian Times.

The locale of the farce is the court of King Arthur; the time, just after the marriage of Huncamunca to Tom Thumb; and the action, the selection of a successor to the recently deceased laureate. The competitors for the honor can be recognized as caricatures of—in addition to Cibber—Lewis Theobald, Dennis, George Ridpath, and Stephen Duck, most of whom in fact had been rumored to be candidates for the laureateship. But Cibber is chosen amid ironical comment on the cultural significance of his supremacy.

Fielding's *Author's Farce* and *Pasquin* also drew on the earlier versions of the *Dunciad*; and Pope in turn apparently took suggestions for his fourth book from these plays.⁴² As first produced in 1730 *The Author's Farce* had as its immediate satirical target Colley Cibber and Robert Wilks, both actor-managers of Drury Lane; but as revised, improved, and produced in 1734, in the version which is now commonly read and with which I shall here be concerned, the play substitutes Theophilus Cibber for Wilks, retaining the senior Cibber.[43] In the years that intervened, Wilks had died and Theophilus Cibber had distinguished himself as a scoundrel. But if the satirical treatment of the Cibbers is both personal and bitter, they are made to serve a symbolical function similar to that served later by Colley Cibber in the revised *Dunciad*: they are types of the theater manager, the dictator of dramatic art in that time of literary depravity, at once perceptive judges of the public taste and headstrong, vain tyrants who pride themselves on capricious conduct.

In the stage rehearsal tradition, *The Author's Farce* presents a playwright and also his play. Luckless, an impoverished youth, hopes to gain solvency by profits from the publication and staging of his "puppet-show," "The Pleasures of the Town." His solicitation of a publisher provides dramatic justification for the introduction of scenes from literary Grubstreet, in which appears a bookseller's manufactory, the workplace of several hacks busy with tasks assigned by the bookseller who has a keen eye to the literary market. Fielding, it will appear, protests the conception of literature as a commodity with a marketable value, suggesting that this conception (held in the play by both the bookseller and the theater managers) is a cause for the prevailing literary degeneracy.

"The Pleasures of the Town" is a dramatization of the *Dunciad*: "The chief business is the election of an arch-poet, or, as others call him, a poet laureate, to the Goddess of Nonsense" (III). Those contending for the laureateship are personifications of the ruling London pleasures. Like Pope, though with far less emphasis, Fielding alludes in dialogue to the increasing prominence of Nonsense (or Dullness) as the extension of the pleasures of the business community to the fashionable end of town: "My Lord-Mayor has shorten'd the time of *Bartholomew*-fair in *Smithfield*," explains a poet to a bookseller (III), "and so they are resolv'd to keep it all the Year round at the other End of the town." Here is an epigrammatic statement of the theme of *The Author's Farce* as well as of the *Dunciad*.

Fielding's *Pasquin* (1736) includes two rehearsals, of a comedy and a tragedy, respectively political and literary satires. It is the literary satire which is relevant here, though it is worth

noting that in *Pasquin,* as in the *Dunciad* of 1743, a judgment
on political corruption parallels and reinforces a judgment on
literary or cultural corruption. The tragedy being rehearsed,
"The Life and Death of Common-Sense," is more starkly allegorical than the puppet show in *The Author's Farce*; it is less
particularized, and it is more bitter. The mock heroics of the
"tragedy," and the comments of Fustian, the author, burlesque
the absurdities of the heroic plays which continued to appear.
But the satire has its center in the allegorical contention of
Queen Common-Sense and Queen Ignorance: in Ignorance's
invasion of the realm of Common-Sense and in the defection of
Common-Sense's followers to the enemy. Prominent among
the deserters are Law and Physic, whose defection occasions
comment generalizing the significance of the tragedy from the
merely theatrical to the universal. Common-Sense herself in-
terprets her fall in terms anticipatory of the fourth book of the
Dunciad (V):

> Farewel, vain World! to *Ignorance* I give thee.
> Her leaden Sceptre shall henceforward rule. . . .
> Henceforth all things shall topsy-turvy turn;
> Physick shall kill, and Law enslave the World:
> Cits shall turn Beaus, and taste *Italian* Songs,
> While Courtiers are Stock-jobbing in the City.

Thoroughly a play about the theater, *Pasquin,* a dramatic
dunciad, reveals the preoccupations of a professional man of the
theater confronted with the conflicting demands of sound critical sense and popular taste in a highly competitive theatrical
situation.

The *Dunciad,* to repeat, is the culmination of a body of
denunciatory comment on the stage, much of it conservative in
social implication. As such this comment represents a supplementary current to the complaints of Jeremy Collier and his
followers, who, as a group, were supported by and associated
with the merchant class. In the morass of early-eighteenth-century dramatic criticism, these two major forces—a moralistic
one leading from Collier and an aesthetic one leading to
Pope—are operative in different, though not opposing, directions.

Perhaps the most striking fact about the stage controversies to a modern student is the volubility of the participants: the sheer bulk of the poems, plays, books, and pamphlets devoted to criticism of the drama. The controversies, moralistic and aesthetic, occasioned a review of the relationship between the drama and contemporary life. "Literary fallacies" inherent in the Restoration tradition in comedy came under critical scrutiny; the rigid set of social values in comedy, inherited from the early years after 1660, were seen to be at variance with the conditions of life. Not that the dramatists forthwith changed the assumptions upon which they constructed plays. The controversies heated tempers, and many playwrights (Farquhar, for example), because they were angry, became more insistent than ever in exploiting class antagonism. But bad temper and aristocratic wit were not enough; times had changed, and the demand for corresponding changes in the drama was too great to resist.

THREE

The Survival of the Restoration Stereotypes, 1693-1710

George Farquhar, in a defensive preface to *The Twin Rivals* (1702), commented on the rigid pattern of expectation against which he and his fellow dramatists wrote. The audience, he complained,

take all Innovations for Grievances; and, let a Project be never so well laid for their Advantage, yet the Undertaker is very likely to suffer by't. A Play without a Beau, Cully, Cuckold, or Coquete, is as Poor an Entertainment to some Pallats, as their Sundays Dinner wou'd be without Beef and Pudding.

"A Play without a Beau, Cully, Cuckold, or Coquete"—or without a knavish citizen or a booby squire—was uncommon at the turn of the century, and was unusual even among Farquhar's own comedies. Just as the dramatic tradition responsible for these character types was pervasive, so was it conservative, inhibiting the readjustment of comedy to the social facts of life. Playwrights were working with stereotypes, most of which were already established—and some long established—in the first decade after the Restoration.

Congreve, Vanbrugh, and Farquhar, the three ablest dramatists writing at the end of the seventeenth century, make little acknowledgment of social changes in their plays, all of which bear the strong impress of dramatic tradition. Their moral judgments sometimes waver, but their social judgments, in comedies intensely preoccupied with social relations, are firm; and the judgments are those of a stratified society. Yet their oversimplification of social fact can be interpreted as an artistic gain in that their plays have a consistency of tone based upon settled opinion. At any rate, the writers of their time who recorded social relationships more faithfully wrote poorer plays.

Congreve, Vanbrugh, and Farquhar were Whigs;[1] but they were Whigs at a time when the party affiliation did not imply sympathy for the business community;[2] they base their plays on social assumptions quite like those expressed later by Swift in the *Examiner*, writing as an authorized spokesman of the Tory ministry led by Harley and St. John.

Even before 1710 several writers—Burnaby, Baker, Steele, and Mrs. Centlivre, among others—wrote plays in which there is a perceptible modification of social judgment: not a decisive shift of sympathy from the gentry to the merchants (as there was in certain plays of a decade or so later), but still a departure from the unyielding assumption that in the antagonism between merchants and gentry the merchants were in an indefensible position. Yet there was not in the years just before and after 1700 a general alteration in the dramatic treatment of social themes. When we come to the undistinguished comedies which then as always formed the larger number of those produced we find a deep and, for the most part, unquestioning conservatism. The obscure dramatists, in their lame and halting comedies, did little more than play variations on a set of conventions, giving no direct attention to the society that was their ostensible subject. Compared with the distinguished comedies of Congreve, Vanbrugh, and Farquhar, most of the comedies of the period 1690–1710 seem poor copies cut to a common pattern by semiskilled artisans.

Except for Farquhar, the dramatists, though they wrote less about rural-urban than about merchant-gentry antagonism, are as conventionally contemptuous of rustics (of country squires and of their families and dependents) as of members of the business community. The dramatic character of the booby squire is formalized (as it was even in Shakespeare's time), and exemplars of the character appear with some regularity. Farquhar's last two plays provide the single instance of appreciative treatment of rusticity; there is in fact no parallel to them until Charles Johnson's work of the second decade of the century.

The seventeen or so plays that Congreve, Vanbrugh, and Farquhar wrote reveal a treatment of class relationships based on a consistent body of social opinion.

In the society these dramatists present, if not in the historical reality, the only "honest" way to an estate open to a gentleman without expectations lies in matrimony. (There are dis-
honest means, such as those attempted by Maskwell in Congreve's *Double Dealer* and Young Wouldbe in Farquhar's
Twin Rivals.) The concentration on courtship, traditional
though it is in comedy, can be seen in these particular comedies
as concentration on the decisive episode in life. For marriage
is the only event the outcome of which is likely to alter in any
substantial way a person's permanent status in a society in which
status is immensely important. Social status and happiness or
unhappiness in marriage are by no means the only things in
life that matter, but they do matter. These plays can end in
marriage with a finality impossible in an age of acknowledged
economic individualism.

Nearly all of the comedies treat problems of love—they
are constructed in terms of a love chase culminating in marriage. Only a few, and those usually sequels to other plays,
treat the affairs of couples already married. But without significant exception, the love affairs are entangled with economic
considerations, very often with the terms of strict marriage
settlements. In this respect the comedies seem to reflect contemporary conditions in a very distinct manner. In the words
of a modern scholar:

Calculations of material interest have played an important part in
marriages between propertied families in almost all periods. But
there is evidence that in the early eighteenth century they were more
important than for the early seventeenth century and for most of
the sixteenth century, and that the material interests involved were
more exclusively a matter of wealth.[3]

In the comedies, as in contemporary life, there were well-estab-
lished patterns of reciprocity in the financial terms of marriage
settlements, and the dramatic characters are forthright in talking about them.[4] When deciding whether or not to marry, the
principals in the love affairs, as well as their older and more
prudent friends and relatives, are acutely conscious of their
prospective mate's fortune or lack of it. A young woman in
Vanbrugh's *Provoked Wife*, in talking to her aunt about the
young man she loves, expresses a common attitude about wealth

and marriage (III): "But if I cou'd make a Conquest of this Son of *Bacchus*, and rival his Bottle; What shou'd I do with him, he has no Fortune: I can't marry him; and sure you wou'd not have me commit Fornication?" She does at last marry him, since she herself possesses £10,000, enough to enable them to live modestly. Without the money, presumably, she would not have married him. In the comedies of Congreve, Vanbrugh, and Farquhar, grossly imprudent marriages do not occur among gentlefolk except where there is trickery. Mrs. Frail in Congreve's *Love for Love* explains to Ben that (III) "marrying without an Estate, is like sailing in a Ship without Ballast."

Wealth is only slightly less important than love as a motivating force in these comedies, and the amount of wealth, which is often in the form of a landed estate, is described as precisely as is the condition of the heroine's affections. Millamant in *The Way of the World* has £12,000 if she marries with her aunt's approval, £6,000 if without; Miss Hoyden in *The Relapse* is heiress to £1,500 a year; Silvia in *The Recruiting Officer* has £1,500 before her brother dies, whereupon she becomes heiress to £1,200 a year; Mrs. Sullen in *The Beaux' Stratagem* had £10,000 at the time of her marriage; Lady Lurewell in *The Constant Couple* has £3,000 a year. The gentlemen who pursue these ladies make no pretense of indifference to their fortunes, which in case of marriage often provide the couple with their sole support, since the gentlemen frequently are younger sons.

Younger sons, in fact, are conspicuous in these plays, having sufficient breeding to be taken seriously, and having the incentive of economic necessity to drive them to lively escapades. A character in Vanbrugh's *Journey to London* describes their plight (I):

What prudent Cares does this deep foreseeing Nation take, for the Support of its worshipful Families! In order to which, and that they may not fail to be always Significant and useful in their Country, it is a settled Foundation-Point that every Child that is born, shall be a Beggar—Except one; and that he—shall be a Fool.

Young Fashion in *The Relapse* courts Miss Hoyden, using his older brother's title, only to encounter awkward situations when his brother appears; and Aimwell in *The Beaux' Strata-gem* assumes his brother's title in his effort to capture a lady with a fortune, learning at the end of the play that he has in-herited the title in earnest. The action of *The Twin Rivals* turns on the efforts of a son, younger than his brother by only a few minutes, to replace his brother as heir. Colonel Standard in *The Constant Couple* is in financial straits because his regi-ment has been disbanded, though he is the younger son of a lord. The hardships occasioned by the principle of primogeni-ture (a common topic in these plays) are suggested by Young Fashion's remark to his brother Lord Foppington in *The Re-lapse* (III): "Oons, if you can't live upon Five Thousand a Year, how do you think I shou'd do't upon Two Hundred?"

The heads of families in these plays have very large in-comes, the size of which is often stated. Lord Foppington, we have just noted, has £5,000 a year; and the elder Wouldbe in *The Twin Rivals* inherits a peerage and £7,000 a year; Sir Harry Wildair in *The Constant Couple* and in its sequel of his own name has £8,000. Sir Paul Plyant in *The Double Dealer*, though he does not cite figures, describes the components of his "plentiful" estate (III): "Why, I have, I thank Heaven, a very plentiful Fortune, a good Estate in the Country, some Houses in Town, and some Mony, a pretty tolerable personal Estate." Presumably, however, he is not immensely rich, as are the lords in other plays, and as is Sir Harry Wildair, who has a lordly fortune. The country squires have smaller, though still large, incomes: Mr. Balance in *The Recruiting Officer* has £1,200 a year; Sir Tunbelly Clumsey in *The Relapse* has £1,500 a year; the father of Lady Lurewell in *The Constant Couple* had £3,000 a year, which she inherited; Mockmode in *Love and a Bottle* has 5,000 acres, from which he derives an abundant income, the precise amount not specified.

We may compare these incomes of characters portrayed or referred to in the comedies with the estimates of incomes made by Gregory King of persons in similar social positions. Tem-poral lords, according to King, had incomes averaging £2,800 a year, baronets had £880, knights had £650, esquires had £450, and gentlemen had £280.[5] These sober estimates of *average* income, it is apparent, are much below the incomes of charac-ters in parallel positions in the plays: the dramatists obviously

exercised their privilege of endowing their characters munifi-
cently. Even so it would appear that the dramatists used some
rough scale of what constituted a fit income for a given rank.
The only character whose income seems totally disproportionate is Sir Harry Wildair—and he is presented as exceptional in
every way.

The social rank of the important characters is most frequently that of the lower levels of the nobility and the upper
levels of the squirearchy: no comedy contains a character of
rank higher than an earl and only *The Confederacy* contains
major characters of rank inferior to the gentry. The barrier between the nobility and the squirearchy is not impassable in these
comedies: there is some movement, and some attempted movement, from one group to another, and members of the two
groups mingle socially. Lord Foppington of *The Relapse*, formerly Sir Novelty Fashion of Cibber's *Love's Last Shift*, has
by means of a £10,000 bribe been made a baron. Sir Tunbelly
Clumsey with his £1,500 a year hopes to marry his daughter to
Foppington and thus ennoble his grandchildren. Mr. Balance
of *The Recruiting Officer* also has ambitions for his daughter
(II): "The Death of your Brother makes you sole Heiress to
my Estate, which three or four Years hence will ammount to
twelve hundred Pound per *annum*; this Fortune gives you a
fair Claim to Quality and a Title; you must set a just Value
upon your self, and, in plain Terms think no more of Captain
Plume." But if lords appear in a number of the comedies, only
in *The Twin Rivals* and *The Relapse* do they appear as main
characters, if we leave out of account Aimwell in *The Beaux'
Stratagem*, who discovers at the end of the play that he has inherited his brother's peerage.

Only Vanbrugh's *Confederacy* has major characters of rank
inferior to the gentry (though a number of the plays have such
characters who appear incidentally). The social milieu of *The
Confederacy* is entirely that of the City, and not even of its
highest ranks: it is that of Gripe and Moneytrap, "Two rich
money Scriveners," of a station distinctly inferior to that of the
aldermen and international traders who appear incidentally in
other plays. Farquhar gives most attention to the society of
the wealthier squires, precisely as do the other dramatists, and
he has no play in which the chief characters are not gentlefolk,

even though he presents some minor characters from humble life more vividly and sympathetically than do the others. Sergeant Kite of *The Recruiting Officer* and Scrub and Cherry of *The Beaux' Stratagem* are among the most memorable figures in comedy of the Restoration tradition: they are fully realized as attractive individuals—Cherry, especially, who offers herself in marriage to Archer with a dowry of £2,000 accumulated by her putative father in his dealings with highwaymen. But characters from humble life always have minor, even if attractive, roles in Farquhar's plays. His important innovation lay not in his treatment of humble characters but in his treatment of rural life—of which more later.

The antimercantile bias of Congreve, Vanbrugh, and Farquhar was such that no attractive merchant character appears in any of their plays (except for one introduced briefly in *The Twin Rivals*). In some plays the merchants are ignored; in others they are the butt of casual but derisive jokes; and in still others they are ridiculed in dramatic caricatures, sometimes very harsh ones. At no time is there an implied acknowledgment of the importance of the merchant and of trade to the nation; on the contrary, there is a tone of contempt for the business community and for the prudential virtues associated with it, which is only occasionally lightened by irony. Even the wit in which the plays abound has a social bias. Wit, as these dramatists understood and esteemed it, was a gentleman's accomplishment, which a citizen could neither practice nor appreciate; and in their comedies they persisted in thinking of merchants as citizens.

Of the three dramatists, Congreve is the wittiest, and the carefully disciplined though metaphorical volubility of his characters makes them by all odds the sprightliest conversationalists of the Restoration stage. In fact, Congreve's sympathetic characters are among the most accomplished conversationalists in English literature; and their conversation is emphatically that of the *beau monde*. In his dedication of *The Way of the World* to the Earl of Mountague, Congreve alludes to his standard for dramatic dialogue:

If it has happen'd in any Part of this Comedy, that I have gain'd a Turn of Stile, or Expression more Correct, or at least more Corrigible than in those which I have formerly written, I must, with

equal Pride and Gratitude, ascribe it to the Honour of Your Lord-
ship's admitting me into Your Conversation, and that of a Society
where every body else was so well worthy of You, in Your Retirement last Summer from the Town: For it was immediately after,
that this Comedy was written.

Congreve overstates the debt, of course; poets are not on their
honor in dedications. But the standard of aristocratic elegance
in conversation here described seems indeed to be the regulat-
ing one in his plays, in all of which the most favored characters
are urbane gentlemen or noblemen who either possess or gain
through marriage a landed estate.

   Of Congreve's four comedies, *The Old Bachelor* (1693)
is the most clearly shaped by social assumptions.[6] The comedy
has three separate actions, each concerned with a distinct social
group; there is some correlation between the characters' social
position and the degree of sympathy or contempt that Congreve shows for them. The admirable characters, the "Truewits" in Congreve's terminology,[7] are Bellmour and Vainlove
and their female counterparts Araminta and Belinda—all members of the gentry, devoted to wit and fun, foes to piety, settled
industry, and rusticity. It is they who dominate the intrigues
and with whom members of the audience are intended to identify themselves; and it is they who are rewarded—by matrimony—at the conclusion. There are two principal characters
who are treated satirically, the one a booby squire, Sir Joseph
Wittol, and the other a City banker, Alderman Fondlewife,
both of whom suffer indignities. Fondlewife, a hypocritical,
Nonconformist banker, is the most harshly treated of the major
characters. Within the satiric framework of the play his offenses (which are made to seem his class's offenses) of hypocrisy, jealousy, and uxoriousness are more harshly regarded than
is the adultery of Bellmour, which seems even to be condoned.

   Vanbrugh's *Confederacy* (1705), a play about Court-City
rivalry, is an adaptation of a French play (Florent Carton Dancourt's *Les Bourgeoises à la Mode*) first produced in Paris in
1692. Vanbrugh followed his original closely, even to many
details of the dialogue, changing the locale, however, to London and making the characters English. His play can be considered a commentary on English society even though it is an
adaptation, because he obviously chose his original for its rele-

vance to the English scene and further reworked it in English terms.

The Confederacy abounds in comic situations; it has a vivacity that saves it from mere sordidness; but the world of vice it portrays precludes lightness of tone. The confederacy of the title is that of the wives of Gripe and Moneytrap to entice each other's husband, with mutual consent, as a means of getting money to support their social pretensions, which include the fashionable vice of gambling. With its central situation of City women aping the gentry, the play resembles many written by earlier dramatists: in its socio-economic values it is not far removed from Jonson and Massinger. Always in the background of the intrigues, determining the direction they take, is the jealousy and envy felt by characters of the merchant class for the nobility and gentry. The City wives desire money for the social opportunities it brings; love and lust for them are but secondary motivations. Court-City rivalry appears steadily, in the incidental conversation as well as in the absurd situations to which the two wives, Clarissa and Araminta, are driven by their social ambitions; and Vanbrugh's judgment, delivered through satire, is emphatically that citizens should keep their places. The drift of his satire is suggested in a conversation between an old peddler and her neighbor (I):

MRS. CLOGGIT: . . . how do you speed amongst your City Customers?

MRS. AMLET: My City Customers! Now by my truth, Neighbour, between the City and the Court (with Reverence be it spoken) there's not a ——— to chuse. My Ladies in the City, in Times past, were as full of Gold as they were of Religion, and as punctual in their Payments as they were in their Prayers; but since they have set their Minds upon Quality, adieu one, adieu t'other, their Money and their Consciences are gone, Heav'n knows where.

Here is suggested the theme of the action to follow.

Farquhar's *Constant Couple* (1699), already discussed in a different context,[8] presents in Alderman Smuggler as bitter a caricature of the miserly, lecherous, and hypocritical merchant as can be found in the whole range of seventeenth-century comedy. But the caricature differs from earlier ones only in its greater harshness and more explicit insistence on hypocrisy. There are the usual two love intrigues in *The Constant Couple*, one culminating in the marriage of Sir Harry Wildair, a baronet with £8,000 a year, and Angelica, the daughter of a titled lady of unspecified rank; and the other in the marriage of Colonel Standard, the younger son of a lord, and Lady Lurewell, the heiress of a baronet, in possession of £3,000 a year. These are the principal characters, all of whom are treated sympathetically. The several prominent characters who are not members of the small circle of wealth, fashion, and quality (of whom Smuggler is but the most conspicuous) are without exception the subjects of satire.

These three plays—*The Old Bachelor*, *The Confederacy*, and *The Constant Couple*—contain the dramatists' most extended and most severe satirical attacks on the merchants; but their other plays contain evidence, even if not such unambiguous evidence, of the same hostility.

No other of Congreve's comedies includes important merchant characters nor detailed treatment of Court-City rivalry. *The Double Dealer* (1693) has only a single intrigue, one dominated by the machinations of an Iago-like villain. The social and economic assumptions upon which the action of the play turns, however, are the traditional ones; and both the prologue and the epilogue contain conventional hits at citizen-cuckolds. Yet Congreve shows himself to be no uncritical lover of quality by his inclusion in the play of telling satire directed at aristocratic snobbery. Mercantile life touches the action of *Love for Love* (1695) and *The Way of the World* (1700) only tangentially. In the earlier play, Trapland, a scrivener who is Valentine's principal creditor, appears briefly to dun him and to be made a fool of—though not to be duped out of his money. Valentine's—and it seems fair to say Congreve's—latent contempt for the merchants comes out in his feigned lunatic ravings when he replies to a question about what will happen in the City on the morrow (IV):

Oh, Prayers will be said in empty Churches, at the usual Hours. Yet you will see such zealous Faces behind Counters, as if Religion were to be sold in every Shop. Oh things will go methodically in the City, the Clocks will strike twelve at Noon, and the horn'd Herd Buz in the Exchange at Two.

In short, just enough is said about the City to establish the traditional attitude of amused contempt. In *The Way of the World* (1700) merchants and mercantile life are all but ignored—there are no merchant characters, and I find only one direct allusion to their class (a conventional one to citizen-cuckolds [III]). The social milieu is that of the wealthier gentry, and it is a milieu inimical to the business community in the premium placed upon wit. The characters, as in Congreve's other plays, are much concerned about money: not about earning it, for that cannot be done in the society in which they live, but in possessing it in the form of an estate.

So too the characters in Vanbrugh's plays. Those of *The Provoked Wife* (1697), to illustrate, belong to the gentry: no prominent character of an inferior rank appears. Sir John Brute, the husband of the "provoked wife," is a gentleman of ample fortune, whose wife married him, he explains (I), for his money; his sottish overindulgence is limited neither by scarcity of funds nor by responsibilities. The other two prominent male characters, Constant and Heartfree, are both "Gentlemen of the Town." Since Constant is involved in an intrigue with Sir John Brute's wife, in which adultery and not matrimony is the object, his economic position has no relevance to the action and does not become apparent except in general terms; but Heartfree wishes to marry Belinda, and the chief obstacle to his doing so is his poverty. He does ultimately marry her, as we have seen, since she has a fortune sufficient to enable them to live modestly. Belinda speaks of her acquiescence with a social realism altogether typical of the play (V):

I can't help being fond of this Rogue; and yet it go's to my Heart to think I must never Whisk to *Hide-Park*, with above a Pair of Horses; Have no Coronet upon my Coach, nor a Page to carry up my Train. But above all—that business of Place—Well; Taking Place, is a Noble Prerogative.

Farquhar's comedies are far more topical than Congreve's and Vanbrugh's. Himself an army officer (as indeed was Vanbrugh), he includes military characters in nearly all of his plays and through them provides comment, always from the soldier's point of view, of England's changing diplomatic and military position. He makes a soldier's matter-of-fact evaluations of international affairs, and only rarely is he chauvinistic. The topicality of his plays—of *Sir Harry Wildair*, for example, which chronicles the first reaction in London to the news of the Spanish King's death, or of *The Recruiting Officer*, which treats with at least poetic truth the problems of impressment in county towns—makes a strong claim on the historical imagination and is, I believe, pure gain. But it frequently crowds out extended treatment of social issues. In *The Constant Couple* only is there concentrated attention to social rivalry. Yet all of his comedies portray a society in which land is assumed to be the proper basis for social pretentions; and in all of them the central characters belong to the nobility or to the gentry.

The comedies of these dramatists satirize absurdities in behavior wherever they are found. Congreve's Lord Froth, Vanbrugh's Sir John Brute, and Farquhar's Young Wouldbe remind us that the dramatists had an eye to folly and wickedness in fashionable life. They were, after all, critics of social behavior rather than of the social structure, which they took largely for granted.

The number of foolish merchants who appear as characters in the obscure comedies produced just before and after 1700 provides remarkable testimony to the public preoccupation with social rivalries—as well as to the capacity of audiences to laugh at old jokes. If dramatic tradition perpetuated the stereotype of the merchant and the plot device of a gallant's outwitting him, still dramatists and audiences alike must have found something timely in these familiar resources of comedy or they would not have been used with such high frequency.

Thomas Dilke's *The City Lady* (1697) presents a representative situation: that of an old, rich City merchant who has been persuaded by his younger, but in this case not very young, wife to move to a more fashionable area. Sir George Grumble, recently married to "A City Lady lately remov'd into *Covent-Garden*, in all things affecting quality," complains that he has had to spend two thousand pounds for equipage to appear in Hyde-Park. Lady Grumble, so says Sir George's brother (I), "who has from her Childhood liv'd in the City, and has been remov'd hither to *Covent-Garden* but a Fortnight, vows already that she admires how a well-bred Woman can take her

Breath within *Temple-bar*." Dilke, like several of his contemporary dramatists, exploits satirically the social penetration of the fashionable areas by rich citizens. The severity of the satirical judgment he passes on Lady Grumble's social ambition is ironically implied in the following remark which she addresses to her husband (II):

Prithee *Georgee* let us consider a little to change our Furniture,—Do you think that City Furniture is fit for this end of the Town?—I have not so much as one Bed with my own Cypher upon't, and I am sure my Quality deserves a Cypher with a Coronet at the head on't, were I dignifi'd suitable to the Grandure of my Soul.

The social assumptions of *The City Lady*, it will be apparent, are little altered from those of the plays of Jonson and Massinger.

In *The Lover's Luck* of two years before (1695), Dilke had shown a more even balance in his satirical treatment of merchant-gentry opposition. Here the antagonism is epitomized in the hostility of two uncles from different sides of the family who are joint guardians of a handsome young heiress. The one, Sir Nicholas Purlew, "a formal Herald and Antiquary" preoccupied with pedigree, chooses for his niece a young fop of more family than intelligence; whereas the other uncle, Alderman Whim, "a Projector and Humorist," chooses for her a lawyer who can assist him in his own multitudinous enterprises. The niece resolves the conflict by choosing her own husband—a brave colonel just home from the wars in Flanders.

Thomas D'Urfey's *The Richmond Heiress* (1693) includes among its characters Dick Stockjobb, "An opinionated impertinent Citizen, a great Stock-jobber," who is an uxorious husband with a flirtatious wife; George Powell's *A Very Good Wife* (1693) has Squeezwit, "A Foolish Citizen, very desirous of being thought a Wit," and Sneaksby, "A Foolish Hen-peck'd City Jeweller," thus described by his wife (I):

Here's my Worshipful Husband, *Mr. Sneaksby*, from a poor Jeweller is come to be a Justice of Peace . . . An Honest Man! he grew to be able to give Six Thousand Pounds with my Daughter, and what as an Honest Man! He bought my Son *Aminidab* a Place at Court, but not by Honesty; what shou'd any one Man do with Honesty, when 'tis enough to undoe a whole Corporation.

Henry Higden's *Wary Widow* (1693) includes a merchant in Sir Worldly Fox, "An *Oliverian* Colonel, a cunning griping Sharper: a Widower, but privately keeps a Mistress"; Edward Ravenscroft's *Canterbury Guests* (1694) presents Alderman Furr, "A Citizen of *London*," an avaricious merchant who has brought his daughter to Canterbury to marry her to a rich country squire. A similar situation appears in George Powell's *The Cornish Comedy* (1696): Gripe, "A Merchant, old, Testy, Lascivious and Miserable," has also brought his daughter into the country to marry her to a squire. Among the gallery of London types in Thomas Dilke's *The Pretenders* (1698) is Broakage, "A poor Bankrupt Merchant, pretending himself to be very rich," who is described by another character ignorant of his true condition as "wonderful rich; . . . He has Colonies in all our Plantations, Cargoes in all our Trading bottoms, and Shares in all our Banks" (I). David Crauford's *Courtship à la Mode* (1700) includes two foolish merchants, both with adjectival names, Sir Anthony Addle and Alderman Chollerick.

Before the second decade of the eighteenth century sympathetic portrayals are very rare indeed; moreover, all three that I have found are adaptations of the work of foreign or earlier playwrights, and reflect to some extent the attitude of the original dramatists. Thus Sir Maurice Meanwell, the honest merchant in Thomas Wright's *The Female Virtuosos* (1693), derives from the corresponding character in Molière's *Les Femmes savantes*; and Mr. Rich, the sober, sensible merchant in Mary Pix's *The Beau Defeated* (1700), presumably has a counterpart in the unidentified French original.[9] Even so, any impression of sympathy for the business community conveyed in the characterization is annulled in the bitter treatment of his sister-in-law, a wealthy merchant's widow bent on social climbing. Joseph Harris's *City Bride* (1696),[10] an adaptation of John Webster's *Cure for a Cuckold*, reveals some sympathy for the merchants, but a joke is made of the fact in the play's epilogue:

> You met with good Intention to be witty,
> And rally the Grave Cuckolds of the City;
> But disappointed of your Recreation,
> I in your Looks can read the Play's Damnation.

Lord! how ye stare to find an honest Bride,
A thing you think a Monster in Cheapside.

If dramatists clung to the merchant stereotype, several of
them at least reveal a neat balance of satirical thrust at both the
"quality" and the business community—a balance epigram-
matically suggested in the prologue to Thomas Baker's *The
Humour of the Age* (1701):

To gain the Court, he calls the City, Fools,
To please the Citts, the Court he redicules.

Indeed he does—and so do Burnaby, Mrs. Centlivre, Steele,
and, in at least one play, Colley Cibber.

The comedies of Baker and Burnaby are undistinguished
if competent in quality; yet they are valuable indeed as a record
of the preoccupations of English society in the opening years
of the eighteenth century, and as an occasionally original commentary on those preoccupations.[11]

Except for Burnaby's *Love Betrayed* (an adaptation of
Twelfth Night), all their comedies give prominent attention to
the theme of merchant-gentry rivalry, sometimes in dramatized
relationships between characters and sometimes merely in dramatic conversation, with a suspension of judgment that is absent
from the comedies of the major Restoration dramatists. To be
sure, Baker and Burnaby satirize the social ambitions of the
merchants, but at the same time they see the substantial nature
of the merchants' claim to consideration and the slender basis
for the gentry's assumption of superiority. All the major
Restoration dramatists ridicule foppery as it appeared among
the gentry and nobility: Sir Fopling Flutter and Lord Foppington were, after all, wellborn. But if Baker and Burnaby
satirize mere foppery, they also include criticism that seems
to be directed at social groups rather than at specific absurd individuals.

Moreover, they are acutely aware of the merchant's invasion of aristocratic privilege. "I don't believe there's an Estate
at Court," observes a character in Baker's *Tunbridge Walks*
(1703) (V), "but is Mortgag'd to an Alderman in the City."
Characters in the plays make repeated reference to the relationship between social and economic rivalry. Lord Promise in
Burnaby's *The Modish Husband* (1702) uses an erotic simile

to point a comparison between City women and fashionable women (III):

Then their Women have the same thrifty principles as their Husbands; they an't for the show of Riches, but the thing! While ours with their Trains of Lovers! Balls, and Coquettry! manage their Pleasures as ill as their Estates; lay it all out in Trappings and Show, and are Beggars at the bottom!

"The Citizens, Madam," observes a gentleman in Baker's *Humour of the Age* (II),

are joyntly busy to cheat all Mankind, and separately one another: They are very Knavish 'till they get Estates, and very honest when they have left off their Trades, and come to be Aldermen: They love Eating and Drinking as well as any People, and understand it as little; and make Entertainments for Quality, to be laugh'd at for their Pains . . . and they take as much Pains to breed up their Sons fine Gentlemen, as if they knew they had Quality in their Natures.

This is the cry of a man who has little but his quality to recommend him.

Burnaby, as well as Baker, presents gentlefolk who are palpably absurd in their affectations—Lady Dainty, for example, a hypochondriac prominent in *The Reformed Wife* (1700), whose disdain for the merchants is only less prominent than her concern about her health. With an ear to epigram and to irony, Burnaby attributes this remark to Lady Dainty (II): "To be always in health is as insipid as to be always in humour; one is the effect of too little Breeding, as the other of too little Wit, and fit only for the Clumsy State of a Citizen." There appears also in the play the familiar coupling of lack of money with the Court, as well as lack of wit with the City. In Burnaby's *Modish Husband*, too, amid conventional talk of cuckolded husbands, occur frequent comparisons of the quality and the merchants; and again the satire is two-edged, biting the gentry and nobility (as groups, not merely as absurd individuals) as well as merchants.

Burnaby's *Ladies' Visiting Day* employs the situation of a socially ambitious wife who has induced her rich and miserly merchant husband to part with some of his City pounds for west end fashion. "What a Pox made me leave *Threadneedle-*

street," exclaims Sir Testy Dolt (III); "my Right Vertuous wou'd have it so; she must be near St. *James*-Park, and *White's* Chocolate-house." Here we have implied the central conflict of this, as of a number of contemporary plays. A variation of this conflict, as we have seen, is widespread in Restoration comedy and occurs even in Caroline comedy, though before the closing years of the seventeenth century few merchant characters appear who have taken up residence outside of the City.[12] Sir Testy, one of the earliest to come, regrets having done so (III): "I have 2000£ owing me in bad Debts, since I came to this lewd End of the Town: If I dun, they threaten to break my Servant's Head; and the honestest of 'em stop my Mouth with Privilege." Conventional and ridiculous merchant husband as he is, Sir Testy makes telling criticism of his aristocratic neighbors. Burnaby makes sport of merchant-class social ambition, but he is, if anything, harsher with the social presumption of wellborn numbskulls. "Really a Gentleman may be sooner known by his Skill in Dress than his Contempt of Learning," comments one character (III); and another (III): "To keep ones word looks like a Tradesman . . . And is as much below a Gentleman as paying ones Debts." These epigrams are too pungent not to function as social criticism.

Baker's *Hampstead Heath* (1705) contains in its gallery of types a citizen couple who are cut to the conventional pattern: Deputy Driver, the husband, a hypocritical Nonconformist stockjobber; and Arabella, a much younger wife who spends her time among the quality. These characters are made to carry a heavy burden of satire, directed at once at the repressive Puritanism of some citizens (here associated with the Puritanism of the Commonwealth—Driver "was the Head of a Faction in *Oliver's* Days" [I]) and at the social ambition of other citizens generated by their new wealth. Driver is not a great merchant but rather a prosperous tradesman, a fact that is driven home to his wife in the course of the action. The intent of the satire is plainly that citizens of Driver's rank should keep their places in the City. Yet the compelling good sense with which Driver speaks about class relationships suggests again the dramatist's suspension of judgment on the antagonism between gentleman and merchant.[13]

Baker's acknowledgment of the important distinction between great merchants and prosperous tradesmen, in *Hamp-*

stead Heath and in other plays, is in fact evidence of the authenticity of his record of the contemporary scene. Congreve and his friends to the contrary, the business community was not all of a piece. "There are degrees in Merchandizing," explains the merchant Nicknack in *The Fine Lady's Airs* (1708) (II), "as well as other Professions. An Officer o' the Guards is above a Captain o' the Train Bands; and, I hope, there's difference between a Gentleman that Trades to the *Indies*, and Merchant *Rag* that sends old Cloaths to *Jamaica*."

The character Nicknack himself is the very personification of suspended judgment. A dandified young merchant, aggrieved that he is compelled to live within the City and carry on his dead father's business, Nicknack "calls himself, The Ladies Merchant; for he imports nothing but Squirrels, Lapdogs, and *Guinea piggs* to insnare the Women" (II).[14] Absurd though he is, however, his remarks often strike home. Consider, for example, the following exchange between him and a colonel from the fashionable end of town (II):

NICKNACK: . . . but why, *Collonel*, shou'd the City be so much despis'd that has so near an affinity to the Court; we have sense to distinguish Men and Manners, Breeding to pay a Valiant Prince homage, that ev'ry Year triumphs for his Country, and generosity to entertain him, where many a hungry Courtier has been glad to sneak in for a dinner.

COLONEL [aside]: The Fellow talks Reason, i'faith;—but prithee, Mr. *Nicknack*, what Business can a Merchant have at this end o' the Town; for a Man that's bred up in a Counting-House to pretend to Airs and Graces, is as monstrously ridiculous, as a Play-House Orange-Wench with a Gold Watch by her side.

NICKNACK: Pardon me there *Collonel*; are Pleasures and Business inconsistent, must ev'ry Citizen be a Drone, that crawls among Furr Gowns, or a Cuckold that's preferr'd by the Common-Hall; pray tell me, what difference is there between a Merchant of a good Education, and a Gentleman of Two Thousand Pounds a Year, only one has Threescore Thousand Pounds clear in his Pocket, and t'other an Estate that's mortgag'd to Threescore People; I have a House in *Billiter-Lane*, the Air's as good as *Pickadilly*. *Cornish* makes my Cloaths, *Chevalier* my Periwigs, I'm courted ev'ry Day to subscribe for singing Opera's, and have had Fifteen Actresses at my Levee with their Benefit-Tickets.

It is important to notice that Baker implies, by way of satire, merely a criticism of Nicknack's personal follies. There is too much obvious good sense in Nicknack's defense of his right to set up as a fine gentleman for the episode to be interpreted as critical of unseemly social ambition. Rather, Baker suggests that the business community could now afford fops—but that merchant fops, like their counterparts among the gentry, are fit subjects for satire.

In so far as the comedies of Colley Cibber, many of which are merely adaptations of older plays, can be said to partake of independent thought, they embody social assumptions not markedly different from those of Congreve. Cibber's plots are the conventional ones of love-game comedy: a group of gentle-born characters, male and female, preoccupied with love, both licit and illicit, pursue each other, usually with some success, through five gay acts. He is much less concerned with social commentary than are Vanbrugh, Farquhar, Burnaby, Baker, Steele, and Mrs. Centlivre. He has less artistic integrity than any one of them; he is more obviously a professional syn-thesizer of plays. Still, he merits some attention here, since he was in closer touch than the others with contemporary theatrical taste by virtue of his association with Drury Lane.

Whatever indication he gives in his earlier comedies of an awareness of the shift in social balance appears in the subjects he avoids rather than in those he undertakes. The theme of social rivalry, of gentleman pitted against merchant, is rare in his comedies; in fact, it is prominent only in his *The Double Gallant* (1707)—and there in episodes adapted from two of Burnaby's comedies. With this exception the character of the ridiculous merchant is significantly absent from his work. As a leading actor, and later as a manager of Drury Lane, Cibber presumably thought it imprudent to offend the businessmen in his audiences, who as a group were becoming increasingly in-distinguishable from gentlemen.

In *The Double Gallant* the characters and situations re-flecting social rivalry are taken over from Burnaby's *Reformed Wife* (1700) and his *Ladies' Visiting Day* (1701). Sir Solomon Sadlife of *The Double Gallant* (Sir Testy Dolt of *The Ladies' Visiting Day* renamed) is a rich merchant who at the insistence of his much younger wife has moved from the City to the fashionable west end (he lives "within three Doors of my Lord Dukes" [III]), only to be tortured by fear of cuckoldom. Treated unsympathetically, as is his prototype in *The Ladies' Visiting Day*, Sir Solomon is an absurd figure, a redaction of the rich and miserly merchant of Restoration comedy. Yet *The Double Gallant*, like Burnaby's original,[15] emphasizes not only the grotesque social inadequacy of an elderly displaced merchant, but the irony of the gentry's assumption of superiority. Among the passages taken from Burnaby is one in which Sir Solomon interviews aspirants to the hand of his wealthy niece and ward. Two of the suitors are impoverished gentlemen; the third is a wealthy merchant who has been knighted. In this scene, intended as satirical commentary on class relationships, the gentlemen are treated as harshly as the merchants— as will appear from the answers the three of them make to Sir Solomon's queries. Captain Strut speaks first (I):

CAPTAIN: I, Sir, am—a Man of Honour.
SIR SOLOMON: Pray, Sir, what's that, a Lord?
CAPTAIN: No, Sir, one that scorns to take the Lye, or pay Debts.

A moment later, Sadlife questions the merchant, Sir Squabble Splithair, who replies:

I, Sir,—am none of your Skip jacks, no spend-thrift Courtier, nor beggarly Soldier, but a solid substantial Man, with a thinking Head, and a prudent Conscience; that have liv'd these 20 Years in St. *Magnes* Parish, have lent my Money to the Government, and owe none of my Neighbours a Shilling.

Sadlife turns finally to Saunter, who replies to a question about his employment:

SAUNTER: Employment! What do you mean, Old Gentleman, Joiner's Work? —Sir, I'm a Gentleman.
SIR SOLOMON: . . . Do you know nothing of the Law, Sir?
SAUNTER: . . . Um!—just as much as I got from being often Arrested.
SIR SOLOMON: Do you follow no Business, Sir?
SAUNTER: No, Sir, I hate it;—I avoid it. —I'll make Business follow me; a Gentleman's above it.

"I see there are other Monsters in the World beside Cuckolds," Sadlife comments at the termination of the interview.

Steele's early plays are of special interest to us here because of his later prominence, in the second and third decades of the century, as a propagandist for the merchants. Certainly he expresses in the early plays none of the conventional contempt for the business community—barring a passing joke in the first scene of *The Funeral* (1701) about the eagerness of rich merchants for armorial bearings. Yet in his first two plays, *The Funeral* and *The Lying Lover* (1703), the business community is almost ignored. Members of it appear prominently only in his third play, *The Tender Husband* (1705). It counts for something, however, in evaluating Steele's early attitudes, that he keeps the easy, traditional jokes about citizen cuckolds out of his first two plays.

That he did so is attributable as much to his sympathy for the dramatic reform movement as to his convictions about social relationships. Steele, unlike Cibber, with whose plays his are frequently associated, went on record for the reformers from the beginning of his career. Whereas Cibber in the dedication of *Love Makes a Man* (1700) and in the dialogue of *The Careless Husband* (1704)[16] refers contemptuously to the reformers, identifying himself (at least in his early plays) with the dramatists under attack, Steele shows sympathy for the aims of the reformers even in his first play, at once avoiding the licentious and profane and calling attention to the fact in his preface. There is, as I have already argued, a meaningful association in Steele's work between his allegiance to the reformers and his respect for the merchants.[17]

In *The Tender Husband* merchant-gentry relations are entangled with the main love intrigue. Clerimont, Jr., explains early in the play (I) that he is a "younger Brother, and you know We that are so, are generally Condemn'd to Shops, Colleges, or Inns of Court"; but since he is of an "Easy indolent Disposition," he would prefer to marry a City heiress—more precisely Biddy Tipkin, the wealthy niece of "an absolute *Lombard-Street* Wit, a Fellow that droles on the strength of Fifty Thousand Pounds: He is call'd on Change Sly-Boots, and by the Force of a very good Credit, and very bad Conscience, he is a leading Person." Biddy herself, a female Quixote,[18] is sharply rebellious against her family's "comfortable" ways. To her aunt's praise of the family's life—"To live Comfortably, is to live with Prudence and Frugality, as we do in *Lombard-Street*" (II)—Biddy replies with a scornful description of the unfashionable thriftiness of the household . Yet Biddy, the most charming of Steele's female characters, can by reason of her innocence and sprightliness scarcely be considered an agent of any severe social satire. The satire inherent in the character does not even remotely take the direction of that in the conventional characters of socially ambitious City women—those in Vanbrugh's *Confederacy*, for example.

In short, the implied socio-economic values of the play (they appear not merely in the pleasantries of Biddy Tipkin but also in the handling of the love intrigue) reveal no distinct hostility to the merchants. The two social groups are clearly defined and their rivalry is central to the play; yet there is no suggestion, through satire, that they should remain apart. Biddy herself, though she lives in the City with her merchant uncle, is the daughter of a country gentlewoman; only by stratagem does she escape marriage to her cousin Humphry, the rustic son of the wealthy squire Sir Harry Gubbin. Biddy's uncle-guardian, a rich banker, has the avariciousness traditional to merchant characters and thus is fair game for the scheming young Clerimont; yet he is no simpleton and cuckold, but, rather, a clever man with a contented wife. Moreover, Clerimont marries, not seduces, the City girl.

The comedies of Susannah Centlivre, one of the most prolific and successful of the early-eighteenth-century dramatists, also represent only a gradual break with the dramatic tradition of the Restoration. They are, in the contemporary terminology, genteel comedies, given over to the portrayal of the love chase, usually of two pairs of gentle-born lovers whose social and financial status is decisively established at the time of marriage. Several of her early comedies include versions of the merchant stereotype, together with the conventional ridicule; however, in her late comedies—in those after 1709, say, when with *The Busy Body* she discovered the possibilities of the Spanish intrigue play—a change is perceptible in social judgments as also in artistic resources. Mrs. Centlivre was thoroughly a professional, much concerned with the money to be made from her plays, and not oversensitive to matters of plagiarism or artistic consistency.[19] She borrowed heavily from earlier plays, both English and Continental, and sometimes she only partially assimilated her borrowings, with the result that we are occasionally in doubt whether in a given dramatic situation we are confronted with her work or that of her original. In her borrowings, as in other qualities, she resembles Cibber; and her plays, like his, reveal perhaps more clearly than plays of superior merit the interaction of a strong dramatic tradition with the new forces in drama. The new ethical thought occasioned an intensified moral earnestness in some of her plays and an intermittent sentimentalism; the Collier controversy and its aftermath occasioned, along with expressions of disparagement of the reformers, a greater restraint in the treatment of sexually suggestive subjects; and the increased importance of merchants in English society occasioned, not an abandonment of the dramatic stereotype, but, progressively in her plays, some modifications in it.

Her most conventional treatment of the merchant occurs in her early comedy *Love's Contrivance; Or, Le Médecin malgré lui* (1703), based in part on Molière's *Médecin*. Sir Toby Doubtful, "an old City Knight," avaricious and lustful, wishes to marry Lucinda, though he is over sixty and she but twenty; and because he is wealthy, Lucinda's father insists on the match. However, Lucinda and Bellmie, a young gentleman of adequate if not extensive means, are in love; and with the adroit help of several friends they contrive to discourage Sir Toby so that they themselves can marry. Their stratagem includes Lucinda's threatening Sir Toby with extensive social activities (IV):

LUCINDA: . . . now I'll prepare for Diversion, and retrieve the time I've lost; you must promise me one thing, Sir *Toby*.
SIR TOBY: What's that, Madam?
LUCINDA: To let me have a House, or very good Lodgings about St. *James's*.
SIR TOBY: About St. *James's?*
BELLIZA [Lucinda's confidante]: Oh! by all Means, Sir *Toby*, all People of Breeding, and Fashion, live at that end of the Town.

Sir Toby is dissuaded from matrimony, as Lucinda wished. The stereotype of the merchant, then, controls the conception

of Sir Toby. Even so, there is no suggestion of social rivalry
between merchant and gentleman. Lucinda prefers her gentleman suitor to Sir Toby, but because of his personal qualifications
and his age rather than his social status.

Like Baker, Mrs. Centlivre sees the important distinction between great merchants, such as Sir Toby, and mere
tradesmen—a departure from the usual practice of the later-
seventeenth-century dramatists. *The Basset-Table* (1705) il-
lustrates this distinction. Prominent among the characters is
"Sir Richard Plainman, formerly a Citizen, but now lives in
Covent-Garden," a rich merchant whose name suggests his
sober turn of mind. Sir Richard is gulled by a young gentleman—in a respectful and forgivable way, however, by the gentleman's marrying Sir Richard's daughter against his wishes.
Among the other characters is "Sago, A Drugster in the City,
very fond of his Wife." Sago is cuckolded; his wife's social
ambitions lead to gambling and near ruin. The dramatist's
judgment is plainly pronounced by one of the characters speaking to Mrs. Sago (III): "Your Husband's Shop wou'd better
become you than Gaming and Gallants." Yet shopkeeper and
great merchant have little in common; there is no suggestion
that Sir Richard should not have forsaken the City for west
end society. His sobriety, mildly ridiculous as it is sometimes
shown to be, appears in favorable contrast with the irresponsi-
bility and dissipation that provide the dramatist's chief satirical
object. Sir Richard, in fact, serves as spokesman for the dramatist's objection to the vice of gambling, which provides the immediate occasion for the didacticism of this play (as in Mrs.
Centlivre's *The Gamester* of the same year). Sir Richard is
made to appear as altogether admirable (and typical of the
Whiggish merchant class) in his fervent support of the war.

Nor does Mrs. Centlivre see anything improper in intermarriage between merchants and gentry. In her *The Platonic
Lady* (1706), in a denouement having some similarities to
that of Steele's later *Conscious Lovers*, the happy discovery is
made that Belvil, a young officer reared on the Continent without knowledge of the identity of his parents, is the son and heir
of a deceased, wealthy merchant, whose surviving brother is a
landed knight or baronet. In *The Busy Body* (1709), though
two exemplars of the merchant stereotype appear—and rather

extreme examplars at that—the two pairs of gay young lovers include members of both merchant and gentle families, with no suggestion of a social barrier between them. This play, in fact, provides an informative example of the coincidence of dramatic traditionalism and altered social assumptions. Sir Francis Gripe, whose very name recalls Wycherley's *Love in a Wood*, and Sir Jealous Traffick, whose adjectival name again is reminiscent of the Restoration, are old, avaricious, and suspicious; and Gripe, a usurer, is also a lecher—scheming to marry his beautiful young ward Miranda. The young lovers are forced to outwit these old men—and they do so handily. Charles Gripe, though Sir Francis's son, is a graceful and accomplished young gallant, an intimate friend of Sir George Airy, who is a gentleman of £4,000 a year. Sir George marries Miranda, and Charles marries the equally charming, and equally resourceful, Isabinda, the daughter of Sir Jealous. The foibles of the merchants thus appear to be occupational rather than generic.

In her *Marplot* (1710)—a sequel to *The Busy Body*, though with a Portuguese setting—Mrs. Centlivre introduces a curious variant on the theme of merchant-gentry relations, presenting social antagonism between a Portuguese grandee and his brother-in-law, a Portuguese merchant. The grandee, having the Iberian oversensitive conception of honor, upbraids the merchant for indifference to his wife's alleged misconduct. As will appear from the following exchange, Mrs. Centlivre has more sympathy for the merchant than for the nobleman (I):

DON LOPEZ [the grandee]: Now, if you don't like the Name of Cuckold, find another for the Husband of a Whore, if you can —For my part I know of none; but this I know, if you won't punish her as a Wife, I will as a Sister; she shall not stain the Honour of my House this way; she injur'd it too much in marrying you . . .

DON PERRIERA: So, there's the Blessing of matching into an honourable Family: Now must I bear all Affronts patiently, because I'm but a Merchant, forsooth—Oh, give me any Curse but this—

The Iberian exaggeration of the point of honor is implicitly criticized; the merchant's healthier and saner conception of personal honor is implicitly approved. The Portuguese are not, in this instance, merely Englishmen with foreign names: an effort is made to endow them with the characteristics of their nation, which was then well known to Englishmen because of the war and because of close trade relations. Yet we may assume that the appearance of the theme of class antagonism owes something to the ubiquitousness of that antagonism in contemporary England.

In the London of Congreve, Vanbrugh, and Farquhar there must have been hundreds, even thousands, of country squires who had come to the metropolis, having invested in joint stock companies, "to be at hand to take the advantage of buying and selling, as the sudden rise or fall of the price directs."[20] The clash between these rustics and their more sophisticated London acquaintances, together with the corollary issues of the rival advantages of country and town, provides one of the major themes of late-seventeenth- and early-eighteenth-century comedy.

The treatment of rural-urban relations in the drama is inextricably associated with the distinction, by no means a clear one, between the aristocracy and the squirearchy. Most of the aristocrats of the seventeenth and eighteenth centuries had country houses and derived a large part of their income from the land. But as a group they were, and indeed still are, as Sir Lewis Namier puts it, "amphibious," having allegiance to both town and country.[21] In the upper classes there were, of course, infinite gradations of rank, prestige, and affluence; and it is impossible to distinguish firmly between the families who could view a season in London as a normal perquisite of their rank and those for whom London was strange and alien.[22] In actual life personal accomplishments, independent of social rank, were no doubt decisive in determining whether or not a man was regarded as a rustic. But in the plays there is an inverse correlation between a character's rank and his rusticity, provided he is not a permanent resident of London. The lords and sons of lords who appear in the plays are never rustics, even though presumably they would live most of the year in the country, but gentlemen of lower rank very often are.

The rusticity of dramatic characters is, then, entangled with considerations of rank. Rusticity itself, implying social maladroitness, is always portrayed as a liability, though it is not always treated with the same severity. Of the three most prominent dramatists writing at this time Farquhar is most tolerant of it, and Vanbrugh perhaps least. Congreve several times caricatures country squires in London; and yet he acknowledges dramatically that sophistication may occasionally be less desirable than rusticity.

Apart from *The Double Dealer*, Congreve includes a country squire in each of his comedies: Sir Joseph Wittol in *The Old Bachelor*, Sir Sampson Legend in *Love for Love*, and Sir Wilfull Witwoud in *The Way of the World*, all three contemptible in varying measure. Sir Joseph is the worst: a dim-witted coward and an easy target for town parasites. Raillery at the expense of the squirearchy appears in the play even in episodes in which Sir Joseph does not figure—as in Belinda's description to her friend Araminta of a meeting with a country family (IV):

BELINDA: Oh; a most comical Sight: A Country Squire, with the Equipage of a Wife and two Daughters, came to Mrs. *Snipwel's* Shop while I was there—But, oh Gad! Two such un-lick'd Cubs!
ARAMINTA: I warrant, plump, Cherry-cheek'd Country Girls.

The tone of these remarks, and of those that follow, provide an ironical reflection upon the "Truewits" themselves. Yet within the total context of the play, a contempt for rusticity is unmistakable. Sir Joseph Wittol is, appropriately it would seem, ingloriously married to the tarnished Sylvia.

In *Love for Love*, apart from the maladroit squire Sir Sampson Legend, who is Valentine's father, a memorable rustic appears in Miss Prue, "a silly awkward Country Girl." Yet Sir Sampson and Miss Prue, though they are duped by town-bred friends and relatives, have a redeeming bucolic charm about them, even if they appear at a disadvantage in repartee. Congreve's preference for town over country appears in his treatment of wit as the accomplishment of an urbane gentleman, an accomplishment resented by merchant and squire alike. "I hate a Wit," comments Sir Sampson Legend about Valentine (V). "I had a Son that was spoil'd among 'em; a good hopeful Lad, 'till he learn'd to be a Wit—And might have risen in the

State—But, a pox on't, his Wit run him out of his Mony, and now his Poverty has run him out of his Wits."

In *The Way of the World* Congreve makes sport of rusticity, and as usual he presents his "Truewits," notably Millamant and Mirabell, as urbane and witty. But he is far from uncritical of the effects of town life. In the Witwouds he introduces a pair of brothers, the elder a country squire and the younger a town-bred lawyer, who illustrate respectively the results of country and town life; and the squire, booby though he is, comes off the better. He has independence, common sense, and courage, though he lacks social finesse; whereas his brother (for whom the family name was apparently chosen) has sacrificed the integrity of his personality to a desire to keep pace with town fashion. However, *The Way of the World*, in its splendid embodiment of wit, must be viewed as one of the most brilliant tributes to urbanity produced by the Augustan age; for wit, as Congreve understood it, is dependent for its existence on a crowded social life such as only a city or a richly endowed estate could make possible. It is inconsistent with prolonged rural retirement.

Vanbrugh is harsher with his squires than Congreve, though he has left a more memorable group of them: Sir Tunbelly Clumsey of *The Relapse*, Polidorus Hogstye of *Aesop*, Sir Francis Headpiece of *A Journey to London*—exemplars of a literary tradition that culminates in Addison's Tory fox hunter of the *Freeholder* essays and in Fielding's Squire Western of *Tom Jones*. These characters are, in their vigorous absurdities, among Vanbrugh's most notable achievements. They lack subtlety, as do all of Vanbrugh's characters, and they do not seem to be the result of considered thought; town and country in fact are frequently opposed in contrasting characters in such a way that the country represents dull virtue and London attractive sin. Fielding, who later saw the antithesis in much the same terms, preferred dull virtue.[23] Not so Vanbrugh; he satirizes both extremes, but his sympathies rest firmly with the Town.

Moved apparently by the emotional dishonesty of the conclusion of Cibber's *Love's Last Shift*, Vanbrugh explores in *The Relapse* (1696) the probable future domestic affairs of a man and wife with utterly different personalities. A source of

strain between Amanda and Loveless appears at once, even in
the too perfect bliss they enjoy at the opening of the play, in
their differing attitudes toward a life of retirement in the country. Loveless's overprotestations of contentment do not pre-
vent Amanda from expressing apprehension at his forthcoming
visit to London (I):

> Forgive the Weakness of a Woman,
> I am uneasie at your going to stay so long in Town,
> I know its false insinuating Pleasures;
> I know the Force of its Delusions;
> I know the Strength of its Attacks;
> I know the weak Defence of Nature;
> I know you are a Man—and I . . . a Wife.

Loveless's subsequent behavior when exposed to the tempta-
tions of London justifies Amanda's fear.

In the second intrigue of *The Relapse,* in which Young
Fashion accomplishes a deceitful marriage to Miss Hoyden,
Vanbrugh confronts country and town in the persons of two
extreme exemplars of rural and urban vices, respectively: Sir
Tunbelly Clumsey and Lord Foppington. Sir Tunbelly, whose
personal qualities are fairly indicated by his name, has £1,500
a year, is a justice of the peace, and is deputy lieutenant of his
county. Although socially ambitious, desiring his daughter's
marriage to a lord (even such a new one as Lord Foppington),
he is laughably deficient in the very social accomplishments in
which Lord Foppington, the stage fop, is proficient to the point
of absurdity—hence the result is the same. In the juxtaposition
of the two caricatures, Vanbrugh exploits to its full humorous
potential the mutual reaction of town and country.

The same rural-urban antagonism is exploited in Vanbrugh's *Aesop* (1697), *The Country House* (1698), and *A
Journey to London,* a fragment about half the length of a com-
plete play, first published by Cibber in 1728 after Vanbrugh's
death. *A Journey to London* presents a particularly choice description of a foolish squire. Sir Francis Headpiece, "a Country
Gentleman" having the foolish hope that he can secure a lucrative place at court and thus repair his fortune, has through extravagant expenditure gained election to Parliament. His
uncle describes him (I):

Forty years and two is the Age of him; in which it is computed by his Butler, his own person has drank two and thirty Ton of Ale. The rest of his Time has been employ'd in persecuting all the poor four-legg'd Creatures round, that wou'd but run away fast enough from him, to give him the high-mettled pleasure of running after them.

. . . His Estate being left him with two Joyntures, and three weighty Mortgages upon it; He, to make all easy, and pay his Brother's and Sister's portions, marry'd a profuse young Housewife for Love, with never a Penny of Money.

In this play as in his others, Vanbrugh is critical of the sophisticated vice of fashionable London; but he shows no inclination to prefer rural simplicity.

Farquhar's last two comedies, *The Recruiting Officer* (1706) and *The Beaux' Stratagem* (1707), the comedies by which he is best known, both have settings in country towns: the one in Shrewsbury and the other in Lichfield. And these semirural settings contribute to the distinctive tone of the plays, the tone of healthy vitality and of easy accommodation to evil that in considerable measure is responsible for their attractiveness. The gang of highwaymen who are associated with Boniface in *The Beaux' Stratagem* are as amiable a lot as Gay's thieves in *The Beggar's Opera* twenty years later.

Farquhar's earlier rustics, however—Mockmode in *Love and a Bottle* (1698) and Clincher, Jr., in *The Constant Couple* (1699)—are less agreeable. Mockmode, the more fully developed character of the two, differs from the dramatic stereotype of the squire only to the extent that he has had a university education. He is an obtuse, yet not unappealing, character come to London to learn to be a wit, who in his determination to acquire the urbane graces must mirror many of Farquhar's contemporaries. "You Country Gentlemen, newly come to *London*," remarks his landlady (II), "like your own Spaniels out of a Pond, must be shaking the Water off, and bespatter every body about you." And his dancing master explains to him (*ibid.*) that " 'Squire and Fool are the same thing here," a judgment in which Farquhar, in his early plays at least, seems to concur.

His last two plays, then, represent a major shift in attitude, a shift away from the traditional contempt for the squirearchy.

In his dedication of *The Recruiting Officer* "To All Friends round the Rekin" Farquhar tells of the circumstances that led to his choice of locale:

'Twas my good fortune to be order'd some time ago into the Place which is made the Scene of this Comedy; I was a perfect Stranger to everything in *Salop*, but its Character of Loyalty, the Number of its Inhabitants, the Alacrity of the Gentlemen in recruiting the Army, with their generous and hospitable Reception of Strangers.

This Character I found so amply verify'd in every Particular, that you made Recruiting, which is the greatest Fatigue upon Earth to others, to be the greatest Pleasure in the World to me.

. . . .

Some little Turns of Humour that I met with almost within the Shade of that famous Hill, gave the rise to this Comedy; and people were apprehensive, that, by the Example of some others, I would make the Town merry at the expense of the Country-Gentlemen: But they forgot that I was to write a Comedy, not a Libel; and that whilst I held to Nature, no Person of any Character in your Country could suffer by being expos'd.

Farquhar distinguishes between stage tradition and contemporary life—in *The Recruiting Officer* and in *The Beaux' Stratagem* as well as in this dedication. If he does not refrain from portraying in Mr. Sullen of the later play a memorable example of the brutish degeneration to which a retired country life can lead, he treats country gentlemen as a class respectfully.

He was too witty a man, and too clever a playwright, to treat rural-urban rivalry soberly, despite his resolution to avoid the caricatures of country types. In *The Beaux' Stratagem* he includes much gay conversation about the rival claims of town and country. When early in the play Aimwell and Archer assess their situation, Archer apostrophizes London (I): "So much Pleasure for so much Money, we have had our Penyworths, and had I Millions, I wou'd go to the same Market again." Town and country provide Dorinda and Mrs. Sullen, too, with a recurrent subject of conversation. "But pray, Madam," Dorinda asks her sister-in-law (II), "how came the Poets and Philosophers that labour'd so much in hunting after Pleasure, to place it at last in a Country Life?" Mrs. Sullen replies: "Because they wanted Money, Child, to find out the Pleasures of the Town: Did you ever see a Poet or a Philosopher worth Ten thousand Pound? If you can shew me such a Man, I'll lay you Fifty Pound you'll find him somewhere within the weekly Bills." Mrs. Sullen is wittier than Dorinda, and her points are more telling; but the argument cannot be won. It is, of course, not the words of any character that establish the dramatist's attitude toward the subject, but rather the total impression created by the play; and in evaluating this impression much must be made of the exuberance of the people who inhabit the countryside. Farquhar surely had some sympathy with the objection expressed by Mr. Balance of *The Recruiting Officer* (II) to the drift of people and wealth to London and its environs.

Farquhar's admiration for the country, as we have seen, was not widely shared at the time he was writing. Other dramatists, including the obscure ones, were customarily as contemptuous of rustics as they were of merchants, and as traditional in portraying them. Thomas Wright in *The Female Virtuosos* (1693) presents a typical pair of rustics in Sir Timothy Witless, "A Country Gentleman," and his son Witless, "A *Cambridge* Scholar," a father and son who bear some resemblance to Steele's later Sir Harry Gubbin and Humphry Gubbin of *The Tender Husband* (1705).[24] Young Witless's rusticity is overlaid but not concealed by a university-acquired pedantry. "A Country Knight that affects to speak Proverbs," Sir Barnaby Buffler of Edward Ravenscroft's *The Canterbury Guests* (1694) is an arrogant and self-centered squire of fifty-five whose £1,500 a year has induced Alderman Furr of London to offer him his daughter in marriage. In George Powell's *Cornish Comedy* (1696), the traditional rustic appears in Swash, "A true Country Squire that makes Recreations his business." Mary Pix's *Beau Defeated* (1700) includes "a Country Squire" in the elder Clerimont "Whose sole delight," according to another character (II), "lay in his Kindred Hounds, who for his Hunting Companions, entertain'd all the Lubbers of the four adjacent Parishes, till the Country was going to Petition the Parliament for Labourers." The anonymous *Intriguing Widow* (1705) portrays in Clodhopper, "A

Country Squire," an extreme exemplar of the rustic, one whose speech is countrified almost to the point of unintelligibility. William Taverner's *The Maid the Mistress* (1708) includes Squire Empty of Essex, whose name conveys an adequate impression of his shortcomings.

Steele's Humphry Gubbin of *The Tender Husband* (1705), the most attractive of the stage bumpkins of the time, is a character exhibiting at once strong individuality and generic resemblances to the stereotype of the booby. Steele seems to have taken suggestions for him from earlier comedies, just as Goldsmith in turn took suggestions from Humphry for Tony Lumpkin.[25] Sir Harry Gubbin, who is the brother-in-law of Mr. Tipkin, the merchant, has brought his son Humphry to London to have him marry his cousin Biddy Tipkin. Humphry, although twenty-three and not without spirit, has been maltreated by his father to the point that he is oafish in his manners and all but illiterate. His trip to London comes to him as a sudden revelation of his deprivation; and he is ridiculous but at the same time appealing as, for the first time possessed of independence, he pursues the pleasures of the town. Finding his cousin unappealing, he marries a tarnished woman, though one of some personal integrity. In depicting Humphry's vulnerability to town sharpers and his naïve delight in London, Steele plays variations on a familiar dramatic theme; but he gives it a remarkable vigor by expending more sympathy than was usual on his rustic.

The Tender Husband is set in London, as are all Steele's other comedies, all of Cibber's that are about English life, all of Burnaby's, and all but two of Mrs. Centlivre's. Baker shows somewhat more variety, choosing as locales such fashionable resorts and suburbs as Tunbridge Wells, Oxford, and Hampstead Heath.[26] Late-seventeenth- and early-eighteenth-century comedy must in fact be viewed as intensely urban; apart from the last two plays of Farquhar's, even in the few ostensible exceptions the rural locales serve primarily as pretexts for sniping at rural life. In addition to *The Recruiting Officer* and *The Beaux' Stratagem*, only Ravenscroft's *Canterbury Guests* (1694), Motteux's *Love's a Jest* (1696), Powell's *Cornish Comedy* (1696), Doggett's *The Country Wake* (1696),

Walker's *Marry, or, Do Worse* (1703), Mrs. Centlivre's *The Man's Bewitched* (1709), and a few others have provincial settings.

The immense growth of London gave a certain timeliness to the jokes about country manners. "Why, the City stands where it did," remarks a character in Motteux's *Love's a Jest* (I), "but the Suburbs are like to overtake you in *Hertfordshire.*" Not quite, perhaps, but the joke had point; and the urban growth which gave it point, as well as the increased prosperity of the business community, had its impact on comedy. After the first decade of the eighteenth century we no longer encounter comedies of the highest quality in the uninterrupted tradition of the Restoration. The narrow conventions of that tradition—in locales, characterization, dialogue, tone, and plotting—had produced brilliant results, departures from reportorial honesty notwithstanding; and it was to be long before any subsequent tradition produced comedy comparable in quality.

FOUR

The End of the War and Change
in Comedy, 1710-1728

In William III's reign and in the earlier years of Anne's, party politics had little discernible impact on the social themes of comedy. Before 1710 or thereabouts, playwrights sometimes expressed partisan political attitudes toward the war and related taxation and made topical allusions with political overtones, but they did not interpret class conflicts according to party principles. The reason is simple: it was not until the political debates preliminary to the Treaty of Utrecht that political rivalry was clearly and emphatically expressed by official propagandists in terms of the central social rivalry in comedy, that between gentry and merchant.

There is a connection between the Whig propaganda of Anne's last years and the shifting social relationships portrayed in comedy in the two decades after 1710. Some earlier plays had implicitly acknowledged the importance and dignity of great merchants, and some had been no more satirical of the merchants than of the gentry. Only after 1710, however, do we find comedies that openly and unequivocally take the side of the merchants.

As is well known, political rivalries in Queen Anne's reign turned on conflicting attitudes toward the war. Although the issues in dispute were far more than exclusively economic, the broad division, subject to many qualifications, between those who supported the war policy and those who opposed it corresponds to the division between the landed and the moneyed interests. The overseas traders and the financiers saw profits that were in the main rising; whereas the landed men (other than the great lords) were hard hit by wartime fluctuations in the price of agricultural products and the four-shilling land tax, so much so that some had to sell their land.[1] It is understand-

able that the squires should have grown insistent that the war
be terminated.

In 1710, the Whig Ministry led by Godolphin, which was
altogether sympathetic to Marlborough's war policy, was dis-
solved—for reasons personal, ecclesiastical, and economic—and
was replaced by the Tory Ministry led by Harley and St. John.
A general election gave the Tories an overwhelming majority
in the House of Commons, a majority consisting mainly of
country squires who were determined that the war should be
brought to an end. The Ministry soon entered into negotiations
with the enemy which, after long delays, terminated in 1713 in
the Treaty of Utrecht.

But before a treaty could be negotiated, it was necessary for
the Ministry to gain popular support for the idea of ending the
war, no easy task in view of the personal popularity of Marlborough and the unprecedented series of victories the English
armies under his command had won. The Tories accordingly
undertook a major journalistic campaign, with Swift as their
leading writer, to discredit Marlborough, the war, and the
Whigs, and to reconcile the nation to the forthcoming peace.
The Whigs countered with a barrage from their own spokesmen: an articulate and pugnacious group of journalists. The
result was extended journalistic debate that canvassed fundamental issues of party policy, compelled individuals and parties
to examine their political assumptions, and articulated the
social and economic rivalries that had been caused by the war.

The antagonisms that pervaded these debates were the
same that animated many of the comedies: the Tory journalists
championed the squires and castigated the merchants and the
"stock-jobbers"; the Whig journalists laughed at the squires
and exalted the merchants as creators of the wealth of England.
I shall take Swift and Addison as representative of the opposing
positions.

Swift in the *Examiner* in 1710 and 1711 insists that landed
interests should take precedence over mercantile interests. He
regrets that the war has had the effect of enriching the latter
at the expense of the former; he expresses sustained contempt
for the financial community; and he emphasizes the value of
high birth, adducing arguments that persons of gentle and
noble birth usually have greater abilities than their social in-

feriors. His sentiments are summed up in the following passage (*The Examiner*, No. 13, November 2, 1710):

It is odd, that among a free Trading People, as we call ourselves, there should so many be found to close in with those Counsels, who have been ever averse from all Overtures towards a Peace. But yet there is no great Mystery in the Matter. Let any Man observe the Equipages in this Town; he shall find the greater Number of those who make a Figure, to be a Species of Men quite different from any that were ever known before the Revolution; consisting either of Generals and Colonels, or of such whose whole Fortunes lie in Funds and Stocks: So that *Power*, which, according to the old Maxim, was used to follow *Land*, is now gone over to *Money*; and the Country Gentleman is in the Condition of a young Heir, out of whose Estate a Scrivener receives half the Rents for Interest, and hath a Mortgage on the Whole; and is therefore always ready to feed his Vices and Extravagancies while there is any Thing left. So that if the War continue some Years longer, a Landed Man will be little better than a Farmer at a rack Rent, to the Army, and to the publick Funds.

Although a prominent Whig and a celebrated author, Addison was not so active in the journalistic controversies as Swift. But he wrote enough on controversial subjects during the last four years of the Queen to establish his opposition to Swift on the issue of merchant-gentry rivalry. Two of the central characters in the fictional circle of which Mr. Spectator is a member are embodiments—controversial embodiments—of the gentry and the merchants: Sir Roger de Coverley, who for all his benevolence is incompetent in practical affairs, and Sir Andrew Freeport, who, if socially deferential to Sir Roger, is clearly the more able of the two. (Addison portrayed Sir Roger more caustically, less sentimentally, than did Steele.)[2] Addison praised the merchants directly, in the *Spectator*, No. 69, eulogizing trade as the source of England's wealth—a theme that later in the century became commonplace but that in 1711 was still controversial. "There are not more useful Members in a Commonwealth than Merchants," Addison writes:

They knit Mankind together in a mutual Intercourse of good Offices, distribute the Gifts of Nature, find Work for the Poor, add Wealth to the Rich, and Magnificence to the Great. Our *English* Merchant converts the Tin of his own Country into Gold, and exchanges his Wooll for Rubies. . . . Trade, without enlarging the *British* Territories, has given us a kind of additional Empire: It has multiplied the Number of the Rich, made our Landed Estates infinitely more Valuable than they were formerly, and added to them an Accession of other Estates as valuable as the Lands themselves.

A forceful statement, in opposition to the Tory view expressed by Swift, and one that was soon echoed in comedy.

Apart from the fundamental issue of ending the war, several lesser issues arose that helped to bring to focus the opposition between the landed and the moneyed interests. One was the Landed Property Qualification Bill of 1711, a bill which with the support of St. John passed both houses of Parliament and gained the royal assent to become law. A Tory measure, designed to keep moneyed men out of Commons and to perpetuate the majority of country squires, the bill provided that, except for the heirs of lords or the heirs of persons with £600 a year in land, no one could sit in Commons who did not have £600 a year in land if a knight of the shire, or £300 if representative of a borough.[3] The terms of Swift's praise of the bill in the *Examiner* establish succinctly the Tories' intent:

The *Qualification*-Bill, incapacitating all Men to serve in Parliament, who have not some Estate in Land, either in Possession or certain Reversion, is perhaps the greatest Security that ever was contrived for preserving the Constitution, which otherwise might, in a little time, lie wholly at the Mercy of the *Moneyed* Interest.[4]

But the measure was not so effective as Swift and other Tories anticipated, for moneyed men found means of qualifying for Parliament through buying estates in fact, or through legal fictions. Addison himself bought an estate that made him eligible for Parliament—and thereby gained the social consequence which, despite all the Whig glorification of trade, went only with the possession of land in the eighteenth century.[5] The Landed Property Qualification Bill, then, failed to perpetuate the squires in Commons, the purpose for which it was intended. But for contemporaries the measure, both in itself and in the journalistic comment it evoked, helped to set in bold relief the opposition between landed men and moneyed men, between gentlemen and merchants.

An issue with similar implications was presented by one of

the commercial clauses of the Treaty of Utrecht, by which it was proposed to resume trade with France, long since suspended for military and economic reasons. The French Commercial Treaty was sponsored by St. John, who hoped to gain partisan political ends by it as well as economic gains for the landed classes of which he was leader. The resumption of trade with France, he believed, would strengthen sentiment in England for the French-supported Pretender; and it would embarrass the English merchant classes by removing the protective tariffs that sheltered them and by interfering with their profitable trade with Portugal. The points at issue were complex, compounded of the economic self-interest of social classes and of political maneuvering in anticipation of the succession to the throne; but in general the Tories supported this clause of the peace treaty and the Whigs opposed it.

The issue occasioned a considerable journalistic debate, in which the principals were Defoe, supporting the measure in a ministerial periodical, the *Mercator*, and a group of prominent merchants opposing it in a periodical entitled *The British Merchant*. Addison, Steele, and others made intermittent contributions to the debate, in which opinion coincided with party affiliation. Despite the Tory majority in Commons, the Whigs ultimately defeated the measure—chiefly because they convinced a substantial body of the squires in Commons that it was unsound in terms of mercantilist economic theory.[6]

The political debates soon had their effect on dramatic criticism, notably in more frequent allusions to the exhaustion of the merchant stereotype. I have already mentioned Addison's complaints in the *Spectator*, Nos. 34 and 446, and the important anonymous one in the *Universal Journal*, July 4, 1724. There are others as well, among them an allusion in the epilogue of Addison's *The Drummer* (1716) to the triteness of jokes about "City-Cuckoldom" and one in the prologue of Charles Johnson's *The Country Lasses* (1715) to dramatists who "in threadbare Jests affront the City." The incongruity between the older dramatic patterns and contemporary fact was becoming apparent.

Hostile treatment of merchants in comedies by no means ceased, but the old stereotype became more and more the province of second-rate dramatists—men who thought of their char-

acters, consciously or otherwise, not as dramatic representations
of contemporary life, but rather as literary conventions that
could vary but slightly from a prescribed pattern. It has always
been so. Not only is it far easier to be derivative than to be
original—especially if one writes in haste, as many of the lesser
dramatists did—but it is easier to see the virtues of the old dis-
pensation than the emerging virtues of the new. The great
Restoration dramatists had seen businessmen as avaricious, hypocritical, and lecherous fools; for their less imaginative succes-
sors, this was enough.

The longevity of the merchant stereotype in early-eighteenth-century comedy owes something to the concurrence of
satirical intent with neoclassical emphasis on generalized characterization. Prefaces and prologues of the day reveal how
steadily the dramatists tried to provide a satirical review of
their times that should be at once comprehensive and corrective.
They espoused a neo-Aristotelian theory of drama, holding
that the didactic function of comedy was best fulfilled by ridi-
culing characters who embodied vices. The neoclassical principle of decorum—articulated by literary theorists like Rymer,
Dennis, Gildon, and Pope—reinforced the tendency to see
social and occupational groups in terms of uniform characteristics. The prologue of William Taverner's *The Maid The
Mistress* (1708) sums up the comic dramatist's role:

> Instructive Satyr shall the Town Survey,
> And draw its Monsters in each artful Play:
> The Fop, the Rake, the Country Squire and Cit,
> The real Blockhead and conceited Wit,
> The Jilting Mistress and the Faithless Wife
> Shall see themselves all painted to the Life.

As the dramatists' hostility toward merchants declined, so
also did their contempt for rustics. Farquhar's last two plays,
as we have seen, depart from Restoration tradition so far as to
portray rural life sympathetically—and other playwrights a
few years later followed his precedent. This departure from
dramatic tradition is remarkable since the tone of English literature around the turn of the century is intensely urbane—more
so, perhaps, than during any other period: this was the time of
the literary importance of the coffee houses, when Dryden held

forth at Will's and Addison at Button's; and this was the time
when the Kit-Cats (Whig poets and politicians) dined at Christopher Cat's, and when the Scriblerus Club met in Dr. Arbuthnot's apartment in St. James's Palace. But the trend was clear,
and as early as 1715, we find signs in comedy of the preference
for country over urban life that is common in English poetry
of the 1740's.

   The comedy that more than any other epitomizes the arguments of the Whig controversialists is Steele's *The Conscious
Lovers*, produced in 1722. The date of production, however,
disguises the comedy's relation to the partisan debates of Anne's
last years, for Steele had already planned it before the Queen
died. As early as June 1710, he included in the *Tatler*, No.
182, what is in all probability an allusion to his plans for the
play; and in January 1714, Swift described satirically the action
of the projected play in such a manner as to suggest that Steele's
plans for it had already been known about London for some
time.[7] Certainly *The Conscious Lovers* as we know it is pre-
figured in Steele's series of major periodicals: the *Tatler* of
1709–10, the *Spectator* of 1711–12, the *Guardian* of 1713, and
the *Englishman* (first series) of 1713–14.
   It is in a special sense a comedy of ideas, of ideas that in
dramatic form were in 1722 fresh and new. Whatever the in-
eptitudes and awkwardnesses of the play, it was in touch with
lively political issues as few others were. Unfortunately, the
ideas are not, for the most part, assimilated into dramatic action
but are rather presented in conversation—with somewhat chilling results. Ponderous expository scenes, resembling *Spectator*
papers put in dialogue, are interspersed with light and laughing scenes, but the juxtaposition never becomes a mixture. The
plot, with its palpable absurdities, is too obviously a vehicle by
which Steele can convey the opinions he formulated in the last
years of Anne, when he was one of the chief Whig propagandists.
   The Conscious Lovers attracted much contemporary comment from literary critics; for the play, the conspicuously successful work of a celebrity, embodies a theory of comedy
evolved in protest against the comedy of the Restoration tradition. Most of the critical commentary, whether sympathetic

or hostile to Steele, turned on principles of literary theory—on Steele's violation of the neoclassical doctrine of kinds by introducing into comedy pathetic incident and characters intended to arouse admiration.[8] But the play also presents the distinctively Whig view of the merchant and of the merchant's relation to the gentry. By way of satire as well as by the direct statements of normative characters, Steele insists on the hollowness of the gentry's assumption of superiority.

A memorandum he prepared while writing the play provides a firm indication of his satirical intent:

> That the Character of Sᵣ· John Edgar [Sir John Bevil] be Enlivened with a Secret vanity About Family, [And let Mʳˢ· Cœland, the March', Wife have the Same Sort of Pride, rejoicing in her own high Blood, Dispising her husbands Pedigree, and Effecting to Marry her Daughter to a Relation of her Own, to take of the Stain of the lowe Birth of her husbands Side, it is Objected, that in the Reign of Edwᵈ the 3ᵈ A relation of her's was a Packer & lord Mayor of London.
>
> The only Scandal to her Family which She Ownes & Cant help, [make Mʳ· Symberton, Such A Sort of Coxcomb as at first Designd Still more Rediculous & Unsufferable from his talents & Improvements.[9]

The subjects of social satire in *The Conscious Lovers* are here suggested: not cuckolded aldermen but family-proud gentlefolk. Steele exploits the theme of social rivalry; he insists on it through repeated allusion; yet he does so with a reversal in satirical intent from that evident in the plays of Congreve, Vanbrugh, and Farquhar. Cimberton and Mrs. Sealand, his two contemptible characters, are of gentle birth; and a special reason for their absurdity is an affectation founded on an assumption of superiority.

The play's central action is provided by the effort of an exemplary young gentleman, Bevil, Jr., to reconcile the conflicting claims of filial devotion and love for a young woman, at first of unknown parentage but ultimately discovered to be the daughter of the rich merchant Sealand. Before the discovery of the young woman's parentage, Bevil's father wishes him to marry another, the known daughter of Sealand and the heiress to a vast fortune; but Sealand, having heard unfounded criticism of young Bevil, is reluctant to permit the marriage.

The two fathers, one a landed gentleman and the other a great merchant, air their differences in opinion (IV):

SIR JOHN BEVIL: Oh Sir, . . . you are laughing at my laying any Stress upon Descent—but I must tell you, Sir, I never knew any one, but he that wanted that Advantage, turn it into Ridicule.

MR. SEALAND: And I never knew any one, who had many better Advantages, put that into his Account—But, Sir *John,* value your self as you please upon your ancient House, I am to talk freely of every thing, you are pleas'd to put into your Bill of Rates, on this Occasion—yet, Sir, I have made no Objections to your Son's Family—'Tis his Morals, that I doubt.

SIR JOHN BEVIL: Sir, I can't help saying, that what might injure a Citizen's Credit, may be no Stain to a Gentleman's Honour.

        . . .

MR. SEALAND: Sir, as much a Cit as you take me for—I know the Town, and the World—and give me leave to say, that we Merchants are a Species of Gentry, that have grown into the World this last Century, and are as honourable, and almost as useful, as you landed Folks, that have always thought yourselves so much above us; For your trading, forsooth! is extended no farther, than a Load of Hay, or a fat Ox—You are pleasant People, indeed; because you are generally bred up to be lazy, therefore, I warrant you, Industry is dishonourable.

The propagandist's willingness to suspend dramatic action in order to underline his points is all too evident in this humorless debate, in which the baronet mouths the clichés of his class, only to have them exposed by the strong sense of the merchant.

If the most celebrated dramatization of Whig argument, *The Conscious Lovers* is by no means the only one. In the larger number of comedies of the period 1710–28, merchant characters, when they appear, approximate the stereotype; but in other comedies merchant characters embody a bias resembling Steele's.

An insistence on the social consequence of the merchant animates a curious comedy entitled *The Beaux Merchant,* published in 1714 though never acted, written "by a Clothier" who has been identified as John Blanch[10]—an empty identification, however, since nothing is known of him. It is only by default of a more accurate term that *The Beaux Merchant* can be called a play, for it is a clumsy piece in which dramatic form is subservient to the intent of praising merchants in opposition to country gentlemen—and of insisting that merchants, too, have a fair claim to the pleasures of polite society. This play, subliterary in quality, is remarkable as the earliest openly propagandistic defense of the merchant in dramatic form: it antedates the production of, though not the preliminary plan for, *The Conscious Lovers*. In it there is a crude and forthright statement of ideas that were later assimilated and more capably expressed by competent dramatists. The play is about the business and love affairs of the "beaux merchant" Harpalus, a character presumably intended to represent an equivalent in mercantile life of the Congrevian man of fashion. There is much circumstantial detail about foreign trade, written, apparently, by someone who understood it very well; and extravagant praise, in terms that were becoming conventional, of the merchant's service to the nation. One of the characters refers, on a representative note, to the landed gentlemen and to "that bitter Edge of Envy, that too much Reigns in their Breast, at the Nice Living and Courtly Behaviour of the Merchant" (I). What the landed gentlemen can do, the author seems to say with a boyish boast, the merchants can do better—even enjoy the town more gracefully.

Mrs. Centlivre's later comedies show an assimilation of Whiggish views in her appreciative portrayal of merchants. A forthright and outspoken Whig even in the uncertain last years of Queen Anne, she avoids the stereotype of the merchant in her comedies of the second decade of the century (as she did not in those of the first),[11] except in one instance in which she presents satirically an exchange broker—as she could do without violating Whig doctrine, in which a distinction was made between speculators, considered to be parasites, and traders, considered to be productive.[12] Her growing emancipation from the traditionalism of her early comedies, evident in her turning away from the characters and situations of Restoration comedy, probably owes something to her increased command of her art. But the modification in implied social judgments can plausibly be associated with the Whig propaganda campaign.

In each of her two comedies of the second decade that were conspicuously successful, *The Wonder; A Woman Keeps a Secret* (1714) and *A Bold Stroke for a Wife* (1718), a young merchant who is socially accomplished appears as the confidant of the chief male character. In her earlier *Busy Body*, as we have seen, the children of merchants are appreciatively introduced as the gay friends of members of the gentry; but the two fathers are but lively versions of the stereotype. By contrast, the stereotype has disappeared altogether from *The Wonder* and occurs in *A Bold Stroke* only in the "Change Broker," who is one in a group of four contrasting social types, all guardians of a single young heiress.

The locale of *The Wonder* is Lisbon, and the characters are both English and Portuguese, the English having been drawn to Portugal by the necessities of commerce and war. The presence of the two nationalities provides an opportunity for contrasting national qualities. Characters make chauvinistic allusions to English freedom, several of them prompted by the observation that Portuguese ladies have much less liberty than their English sisters. There is an implied contrast between the Iberian conception of the importance of lineage and the more liberal English conception. Frederick, an English merchant who lives and conducts business in Lisbon, enjoys the friendship and confidence of the Portuguese grandees, though he is not, to his regret, treated as an equal. A conversation between Frederick and Don Lopez, one of the grandees, establishes the terms of his relationship with the Portuguese nobility, a matter of concern to Frederick; for were his status higher, he could hope to marry Don Lopez's daughter (I):

DON LOPEZ: I am not ignorant of the Friendship between my Son and you. I have heard him commend your Morals, and lament your Want of noble Birth.
FREDERICK: That's Nature's Fault, my Lord, 'tis some Comfort not to owe one's Misfortunes to one's self, yet 'tis impossible not to regret the Want of noble Birth.
DON LOPEZ: 'Tis pity indeed such excellent Parts as you are Master of, should be eclipsed by mean Extraction.

When he is left alone, Frederick in a soliloquy alludes to his love for the nobleman's daughter, concluding on a note of resignation: "But a Merchant, and a Grandee of *Spain*, are inconsistent names—" And with that remark the subject is permanently dropped. If, then, there is no insistence on the social deserts of the merchants, there is a favorable characterization of one, and an implied contrast between the inflexible social structure of Portugal and the more flexible one of England.

Cibber shows a change in attitude toward the merchants parallel to that of Mrs. Centlivre. He had been restrained in his use of the stereotype even in his early plays; yet in those written before the death of Queen Anne, he expends little sympathy on characters not members of the landed gentry or nobility. Among his characters in *The Refusal* (1721) is a rich citizen and South Sea director, Sir Gilbert Wrangle, a stereotype in some ways but essentially an attractive figure, aligned with, rather than opposed to, the gay young gallants in the love intrigue. Although *The Refusal* is an adaptation of Molière's *Les Femmes savantes*,[13] we can assume that the conception of Sir Gilbert Wrangle is Cibber's own because of the topical nature of the action in which he is central.

The time of the action is the peak of the South Sea Bubble— the summer, say, of 1720—when South Sea stock sold for a thousand pounds a share. It is indeed the immense inflation of the stock that has occasioned the complication of the love intrigue: when the stock was low Sir Gilbert, following an argument, became party to a wager with Witling, a fop, on what Sir Gilbert regarded as a certainty—that the stock would not reach a thousand. Witling, having won the wager as well as a huge fortune in stock, demands Sir Gilbert's compliance with the terms: Sir Gilbert's approval for his marriage with either of Sir Gilbert's handsome daughters. Bound by his sense of honor to observe the terms of the wager, Sir Gilbert can only hope that Granger and Frankly, two young gentlemen who are suitors for his daughters, will with the girls' contrivance be successful—as of course they are, one of the girls inducing Witling to give up Sir Gilbert's "promissory note."

Here is a merchant interpreted in an altogether new way. Sir Gilbert has through a foolish wager placed his daughters in a difficult position; but he made the wager as a man of spirit, in an effort to oppose folly. Having made it and lost, he feels bound to fulfill punctiliously the prescribed terms. In a conversation with Frankly (III), he explains his motives and congratulates himself on his status as a merchant—with borrowings from the Whig propagandists and anticipations of Mr. Sealand in Steele's *Conscious Lovers*, produced the next year:

SIR GILBERT: . . . I have taken the Premium, and must stand to my Contract. For let me tell you, Sir, we Citizens are as tender of our Credit in *Change-Alley*, as you fine Gentleman are of your Honour at Court.

FRANKLY: Sir, depend upon it, your Credit shall not suffer by me, whatever it may by your Comparison.

SIR GILBERT: Why, what ails the Comparison? Sir, I think the Credit of the City may be compared to that of any Body of Men in *Europe*.

FRANKLY: Yes, Sir; but you mistake me: I question if any Bodies may be compared to that of the City.

SIR GILBERT: O! your humble Servant, Sir; I did not take you— . . . You'll find 'tis not your Court, but City-Politicians must do the Nation's Business at last. Why, what did your Courtiers do all the two last Reigns, but borrow Money to make War? and make War to make Peace, and make Peace to make War? And then to be Bullies in one, and Bubbles in t'other? A very pretty Account truly; but we have made Money, Man: Money! Money! there's the Health and Life-Blood of a Government: And therefore I insist upon't, that we are the wisest Citizens in *Europe*; for we have coin'd more Cash in an Hour, than the Tower of *London* in twenty Years.

FRANKLY: Nay, you govern the World now, it's plain, Sir; and truly that makes us hope it's upon the mending hand: For since our Men of Quality are got so thick into *Change-Alley*, who knows but in time a great Man's Word may go as far as a Tradesman's?

SIR GILBERT: Ah! a Wag! a Wag!

There is banter here, of course, and overstatement intended as mild irony. But the humor of the conversation serves to make palatable the praise of the merchants, which would otherwise seem intrusive in a gay comedy.

Sir Gilbert, even though a South Sea director, is portrayed sympathetically to the end. He is astonished and annoyed by the fever of stockjobbing, though he has profited from it, and he closes the play with the wise advice to all about him to sell their stock for ready money. Cibber, after all, produced the play several months after the crash.[14]

Steele, Mrs. Centlivre, and Cibber, the most distinguished playwrights in the interval between *The Beaux' Stratagem* (1707) and *The Beggar's Opera* (1728), were, then, thorough Whigs in their interpretation of the merchant. In contrast, almost all the petty dramatists of these years hewed to the old traditions. These dramatists, several of them actors by profession, who wrote one, two, or three indifferent comedies or farcical afterpieces, turned variations on the stereotype, making no dramatic acknowledgment of the distinctions between occupations and levels of attainment in business life. "Usurers," tradesmen, stockjobbers, bankers, merchants in domestic trade, and merchants in foreign trade all are introduced indifferently as variants in a character not much altered from Wycherley's time. Thus there seems to be some positive correlation between the literary merit of comedies produced during these years and the more liberal social views.

Newburgh Hamilton's *The Petticoat-Plotter* (1712), a farce in two acts that was popular enough to be acted for several years, has characters and action with a simplicity suggestive of the allegorical patterns of a morality play.[15] Mr. Thrifty, a merchant, is impelled by avarice to insist that his daughter Isabella marry Sir Simon Scrape-all, a seventy-year-old "usurer," rather than True-love, a worthy and resourceful, if poor, young man, with whom Isabella is in love. The course of True-love does not run smooth, but he prevails handily.

The outwitting of a foolish merchant provides the subject of another farce three years later, Benjamin Griffin's *Love in a Sack* (1715). Sir Arthur Addlepate, an old citizen now resident in Covent Garden, has fallen absurdly in love with the young wife of an officer, Captain Debonair. His servant cautions him about the danger of an amour (I):

You know the Character you have about Town of a grave, sober, discreet Magistrate, an unweary'd Opposer of Lewdness and Debauchery; and then you, Sir, that have so often scoured the whole Parish of *Covent-garden* to clear it of Whores, and whipt all from the Velvet-Scarf to the three-penny Flat-Cap, to be catch'd at last in a Petticoat-Plot yourself, would ruin your Credit for ever.

Sir Arthur nevertheless pursues the young wife, who, urged on by her husband and friends (including a young man who loves Sir Arthur's daughter), leads him into a compromising position from which she releases him only when he agrees to let the young man marry his daughter.

William Taverner's *The Female Advocates; Or, The Frantic Stock-Jobbers*, first acted in 1713 though it was altered from an earlier, unacted play of 1705,[16] has a more fully developed though not much more subtle intrigue: a young couple in love scheme to frustrate the plan of the young woman's guardian to marry her to an old but rich citizen, so that they can themselves be married. Sir Charles Transfer, the young woman's guardian, and Sir Feeble Dotard, the husband her guardian has selected for her, are merchants whose avarice and hypocrisy occasion righteous denunciation, at length, by the young gentlemen of the play. Reinforcing the merchant-gentry antagonism, in this play which was produced the year of the Treaty of Utrecht, there is also a note of antagonism between soldier and civilian, between the officer, Captain Stanworth, who at high personal cost contributed to the victory, and the merchant, Sir Charles Transfer, who, having profited from the war, despises the soldiers who suffered for the nation.

Taverner again in *The Artful Wife* (1717) treats class rivalries and mutual resentments satirically, though this time with a certain subtlety. A lord's household is the scene of the action, and, with one exception, all of the principal characters are members of the nobility or gentry. The one exception is Ruth, the niece of the lord's wife, who notwithstanding her relationship (by her aunt's marriage) to a peer, is a City girl, by temperament and manners as well as by upbringing. Her presence provides occasion for extended talk about the rival merits of the east and west ends of London. "There's Lady *Harriet* and Mrs. *Ruth* engag'd in a warm Argument," observes Sir Francis Courtal (II), whose surname describes him. "St. *James*'s and the City are the Foundation. No two Councils at the Bar ever wrangled more to support their contrary Opinions." The portrait of Ruth is satirical yet not unsympathetic: she is absurd in her devotion to the City, and she is a hypocrite; but she is shown to be a wronged girl, seduced by the experienced and unscrupulous Courtal, whom she loves. Her loss of

honor is ultimately amended by Courtal's enforced marriage
to her. The qualified sympathy expended on Ruth, however,
fails to alter the impression of contempt for the City conveyed
by the sustained sarcastic comments of several characters.

All three of Charles Molloy's plays satirize the citizens.
In *The Perplexed Couple; Or, Mistake upon Mistake* (1715)
there are no fewer than three representatives of the avaricious
old merchant: Morecraft, the heroine's father; Sterling, "an
old Usurer" to whom Morecraft wishes to marry his daughter;
and Sir Anthony Thinwit, "a Citizen," married to a young
woman whose "Visitors are People of Fashion, fine bred Folks"
(II). The main plot is provided by a young gentleman's successful stratagem to marry Morecraft's daughter over his objections; and the subplot by the marital misadventures of Sir
Anthony Thinwit. *The Half-Pay Officers* (1720), a farce that
is little more than a pastiche of several earlier plays (*Henry V*,
Much Ado About Nothing, and Davenant's *Love and Honour*),[17] includes as one of several lines of action a competition
between two absurd citizens, Meagre, "a Scrivener," and Load-
ham, "a *Hamburgh* Merchant," for a handsome young heiress,
who laughs at them and will have neither of them. *The Coquet; Or, The English Chevalier* (1718), an intrigue play in
the Spanish manner, has a French locale, a circumstance that
permits the introduction of generalized conversation about
England—some of it criticism of the business community.

James Moore-Smythe's *The Rival Modes* (1727), a "genteel" comedy given over to the love chase of two gay couples,
includes class antagonism as a subsidiary theme, introduced
not in dramatic action but rather in conversational allusion.
The dramatist's social judgments, as they appear in the handling of characters, intrigue, and satire, are more subtle than
usual, at times even ambiguous, but still fundamentally conservative. Of the two handsome young women who are pur-
sued by suitors, the wittier and more attractive is the wealthy
widow of a London merchant. Not herself a person of quality,
as she freely acknowledges, she nevertheless avoids her late
husband's merchant relatives; and she considers marriage to a
titled husband. Her maid comments (II):

Well, 'tis a Blessing upon your Ladyship's Endeavours, that you
need not give yourself much Fatigue in finding out such a Person,

tho' I don't doubt your Industry after you're set upon it;—but the Question is, whether you would chuse a Coach with a Coronet, or with Horses?

The jokes about the quality are reinforced dramatically by the inclusion among the characters of two foppish lords, father and son, old and young variants of the stock character of the beau. Their comments, again, turn to the theme of the poverty of the fashionable world. "A Person of Quality never pays ready Money but at a Turnpike," observes the father, Lord Late-Airs, on a familiar note (III).

The Rival Modes was produced at Drury Lane, but most of the other plays here described as embodying the older dramatic conception of the merchant were produced at Lincoln's Inn Fields (i.e., at the "new" theater which opened in 1714). During the years in question only one new play produced at Lincoln's Inn Fields, Elkanah Settle's *The Lady's Triumph* (1718) (about a young wife's duping a knight who attempts to seduce her), includes a sympathetic portrayal of a merchant—and this one includes also a pointed observation that a good and generous merchant is a rare exception. At Drury Lane, by contrast, the merchant stereotype was rarely in evidence in the new plays, and there were several sympathetic and original portrayals of merchants: in Mrs. Centlivre's *The Wonder* and *A Bold Stroke for a Wife*, Cibber's *Refusal*, and Steele's *Conscious Lovers*.

There are two reasons, I believe, for the difference in the theaters' records. First, Drury Lane during the reign of George I was ostentatiously Whiggish: as I have elsewhere argued, its managers, with Steele as titular head, attempted to identify the theater with the victorious Whigs and to identify their rivals at Lincoln's Inn Fields with the discredited Tories.[18] There seems in fact to have been some disaffection to George I at Lincoln's Inn Fields. It is scarcely plausible that at either theater political theory could have determined managerial policy to the extent that the managers would have been sympathetic or hostile to comedies depending on dramatized attitudes of social philosophy; but it is not implausible that Whig dramatists, whose social views influenced their comedies, would have been attracted to Drury Lane and Tory dramatists to Lincoln's Inn Fields. Second, during most of these years Drury Lane was the more prosperous theater: it had a better management and a stronger company of actors, and it usually was the more popular with the public. Thus, one season with another, the better plays were produced at Drury Lane and the poorer at Lincoln's Inn Fields; and among the poorer comedies certainly were those that included such stock situations as the outwitting of foolish merchants.

The frenzy of interest in stockjobbing occasioned by the South Sea Bubble provoked considerable dramatic commentary, all of it hostile to the speculators. Stockjobbers were familiar targets of abuse in drama long before the Bubble, and the absurdities of speculation engendered by the Bubble could but intensify the animus of dramatic satirists against them. Because dramatists often neglected to make occupational distinctions among businessmen, resentment of the Bubble sometimes seems to be generalized in the dramatic portrayal of the business community as a whole. The South Sea disaster was, after all, a financial one, made possible by the relative strengthening of the moneyed interest over the landed; it was a very caricature of the social forces that conservatives despised. Stock speculation offered quick wealth, quick poverty, insecurity, uncertainty—in brief, a sudden overthrowing of the social and economic boundaries of English life. "How long have you been a Gentleman?" asks one character of another in an unacted farce of 1720. And the successful speculator answers: "About a Week, Madam."[19] Whig theorists, to be sure, distinguished between the function of the merchant, assumed to be constructive, and the function of the stockjobber, assumed to be parasitical. Steele in the *Englishman* (first series), No. 4, October 13, 1713, joins eulogy of the one with denunciation of the other:

When I am giving my Thoughts a Loose in the Contemplation of the Ways of Men, there is no Man whom I so highly honour as the Merchant. This is he who turns all the Disadvantages of our Situation into our Profit and Honour. His Care and Industry ties his Country to the Continent, and the whole Globe pays his Nation a voluntary Tribute due to her from his Merit. His Hand-writing has the Weight of Coin, and his good Character is Riches to the rest of his Countrymen. All other Subjects of our Island, from the highest to the lowest, are as much below the Merchant in political Merit, as that ravenous Worm in the Entrails of the State the Stock-Jobber.

Some dramatists, especially the Whigs, distinguish between merchants and stockjobbers, portraying the one sympathetically and the other satirically. Mrs. Centlivre makes this distinction in *A Bold Stroke for a Wife*, and Cibber makes something like it in *The Refusal*. But Whig and Tory agreed in denouncing the stockjobbers: the drama of a decade before and a decade after the South Sea Bubble contains satirical caricatures of them and allusions to the speculation that they encouraged. In Charles Johnson's *The Country Lasses* (1715) a misanthropic character, on a typical note, includes as an item in his arraignment of London the refinement in financial procedure (I): "And instead of changing honest Staple for Gold and Silver, you deal in Bears and Bulls only." And in Charles Molloy's *Coquet* (1718) a French gentleman describes stockjobbers as (II) "a set of Juglers that flock about that Pile of Building call'd the Exchange, who get great Estates by buying and selling nothing."

The allusions to speculation in stocks understandably become more numerous and more bitter in comedies of 1720, when the boom and bust in South Sea stock occurred, and in those of the years just after. The best play satirizing the South Sea madness, though not the most bitter, is Cibber's *Refusal* (1721), which I have already discussed in a different connection. His tone of gay amusement notwithstanding, Cibber conveys an impression of the bewildering dislocation of London society caused by the South Sea phenomenon.

The wave of speculation occasioned a spate of farces, only two of which, however, seem to have been acted: Thomas Odell's *The Chimera* (1721) and Francis Hawling's *It Should Have Come Sooner; Or, The Historic, Satiric, Tragi-Comic Humours of Exchange Alley* (1723). Since the latter apparently was not printed, we can merely surmise its nature from the descriptive title. *The Chimera* is a farce about the schemes and subsequent apprehension and arrest of the projectors of a bubble. The names and descriptions of the *dramatis personae* give an accurate impression of the farce's satirical intent: Lord

Gracebubble, "chose Governour of a Bubble to give it a Sanction"; Selfroth, "the Projector"; Hide-and-Seek, "a Banker, a Director"; Sir Nicholas Ninnyhammer, "a Country Gentleman, come to Town to sell his Estate"; Snap, "a Stock-Jobber"; among others. William Rufus Chetwood's *The Stock-Jobbers; Or, The Humours of Exchange-Alley* (1720), the anonymous *Exchange-Alley; Or, The Stock-Jobber Turned Gentleman, with the Humours of our Modern Projectors* (1720), *The Broken Stock-Jobbers; Or, Work for the Bailiffs* (1720), and *The Modern Poetasters; Or, Directors no Conjurors* (1725) are unimportant and unacted farces, the first two having some small merit, the next less, and the last none. Their themes are the same: the insanity of the current interest in speculation. In other plays there is brief allusion to the Bubble: in Sandford's *The Female Fop* (1723), for example, there is a reference to imaginary South Sea gold (I); and as late as Fielding's *The Modern Husband* (1732) the title character's financial difficulties are attributed to losses in the "*South-Sea*, and others" (I).

The Bubble thus made a deep impression on the dramatists. Many it simply reinforced in their conservative distrust of the business community; they now make fun of stockjobbers, as they had once made fun of shipowners and shopkeepers. But there was another, perhaps more important, consequence for comedy. As we have seen, Defoe attributed the expansion of London partly to the need of gentlemen to be at hand to take advantage of the rise or fall of stocks. Disillusionment in speculation understandably turned some men's attention back to the country, just as the disaster of the Bubble made investment in land, as opposed to investment in stocks, more attractive.[20] It is therefore plausible that the Bubble disaster contributed to the shift of literary interest from London to the country that begins to be apparent in the 1720's and becomes marked in the 1740's. Whatever the reason, dramatists began to look more frequently to the country for the settings of their comedies.

As early as 1715 and 1716, two new plays were produced that have something of the rural freshness of Farquhar's *Recruiting Officer* and *Beaux' Stratagem*—Addison's *Drummer* and Johnson's *Country Lasses*, set respectively in a country mansion and in the vicinity of one.

Since Addison never acknowledged *The Drummer* (1716), which had only an indifferent success when first produced, there is some lingering doubt that he wrote it, despite Steele's assertion that he did so.[21] Probably Steele was right: the chaste tone of the play and an outspoken defense of Christianity against "freethinkers" embedded in the dialogue are consistent with Addison's known attitudes. A critic writing in the *Freeholder's Journal*, February 7, 1722, even professed to see in "the Characters and Sentiments" a "Transcript of several in the Spectator." The question of authorship apart, the comedy was asserted (in its epilogue) to be a departure from dramatic tradition:

> Void as it is of all the usual Arts
> To warm your Fancies, and to steal your Hearts:
> No Court-Intrigue, Nor City-Cuckoldom,
> No Song, no Dance, no Musick—but a Drum—
> No smutty Thought in doubtful Phrase exprest;
> And, Gentlemen, if so, pray where's the Jest?
>
> . . .
>
> Too long has Marriage, in this tasteless Age,
> With ill-bred Raillery supply'd the Stage;
> No little Scribler is of Wit so bare,
> But has his fling at the poor Wedded Pair;
> Our Author deals not in Conceits so stale. . . .

There are no gay couples in pursuit of each other, no wit duels, and only one stock character, a fop named Tinsel; and the rural setting emphasizes the break with tradition. The play is in fact a ghost story humorously dramatized: about a husband's sly return to his wife and his estate after having been reported killed in battle. Both the husband and the wife are portrayed as morally admirable, humorous but disinclined toward the frivolity satirized in the character Tinsel, who, as one evidence of his foppishness, disparages life in the country (I): " 'Tis the Solitude of the Country that creates these Whimsies; there was never such a thing as a Ghost heard of at *London*, except in the Play-house. . . . 'Tis the Scene of Pleasure and Diversions, where there's something to amuse you every Hour of the Day. Life's not Life in the Country." The husband and wife, more sensibly, are content on their estate: the play closes with the husband joyfully exhibiting his bounty as a squire.

Charles Johnson's *Country Lasses* (1715) is more explicitly than *The Drummer* an exposition of the charm of country life. The theme of country against town pervades the comedy, and Johnson's later comedies as well. Based in part on Fletcher's *The Custom of the Country* and Middleton's *A Mad World, My Masters*,[22] *The Country Lasses* is an attractive play about a country romp of two young gentlemen, Heartwell and Modely, and their courtship of two young gentlewomen, Flora and Aura, whom they mistakenly take to be village lasses. From the opening scene, the conversation turns on the rival merits of London and the country, Heartwell defending the town, Modely the country; Aura the town, Flora the country; and Freehold, Aura's father, uttering denunciations of urban life in the vein of the Latin satirists whom he reads. "I hear what your Modern London is," comments Freehold (I). "We were Lewd indeed in our Days, but then even Lewdness had Propriety; but of late they say your Fools set up for Rakes, and Rakes for Politicians." The astringency of his comments and the raillery of the young couples give the play a satirical edge that is not destroyed by its sentimental episodes.

Johnson's afterpiece *The Cobbler of Preston* (1716), a Whiggish satire on the recent Jacobite uprising, is an adaptation of the Christopher Sly episode in *The Taming of the Shrew*—in Johnson's version poor befuddled Sly having been seduced to the cause of the Pretender by the October ale of the local Jacobites. Although his choice of locale was determined by the contemporary interest in Preston Heath, where the Jacobite rebels had just been captured, he takes advantage of the rural setting to depict the joys of life in a manor house. In 1723 he produced *Love in a Forest*, an adaptation of *As You Like It*—again demonstrating his esteem for life in the country. In 1729, following Gay's precedent, he produced a ballad opera, *The Village Opera*, a gay and charming piece on a rustic theme. His last play, *Caelia; Or, The Perjured Lover* (1732), a tragedy, portrays wickedness and degeneracy in London even more bitterly than Fielding's *Modern Husband* (1732) and the third part of his novel *Tom Jones*.

In the first ten years of George I's reign, political subjects were exploited in several other farces and comedies with rural locales. One was another *Cobbler of Preston*, a weak, clumsy farce written by Christopher Bullock for Lincoln's Inn Fields to anticipate Johnson's farce at Drury Lane.[23] A more interesting one, but one not produced because the Master of the Revels would not license it, was Mrs. Centlivre's *The Gotham Election* (published in 1715).[24] This short play, which like Fielding's *Don Quixote in England* (1734) and the comedy "rehearsed" in his *Pasquin* (1736) is a farcical treatment of a corrupt election, contains a group of brisk portraits of local types. Far indeed from idealization of life in a village, the play nevertheless portrays with affectionate gusto local characters going about their daily affairs.

Benjamin Griffin's *Whig and Tory* (1720) and John Sturmy's *The Compromise; Or, Faults on both Sides* (1722), full-length comedies with country locales, both use political rivalries as complications in love intrigues. Each presents two headstrong squires of opposite political principles whose dislike for each other on political grounds provides an obstacle to the marriage of their children or wards. The old gentlemen— all of them, perhaps, except Sir Rowland Heartfree, the Whig in *Whig and Tory*—are variants of the traditional character of the squire, gentlemen whose intelligence, already limited, is obscured by obstinacy and prejudice. Sturmy in *The Compromise* exploits the country locale more fully than Griffin in *Whig and Tory*, who indeed uses it as a mere backdrop for a comedy of love intrigue with epigrammatic dialogue after the manner of Congreve. In *The Compromise*, on the other hand, local customs and characters appear prominently, and the election of a mayor, with the customary pre-election campaigning, is entangled with the love intrigue. Neither play had notable success, or deserved to have it. They are of interest primarily as suggesting that the contemporary obsession with politics, and the consequent interest in rural elections where control of the House of Commons was determined, had something to do with the turn of theatrical attention to the country.

Several other plays produced during the reign of George I, though devoid of extended talk of politics, have rural locales and include humorous portrayals of rustic customs and character types: Mary Davys' *The Northern Heiress; Or, The Humours of York* (1716), Captain John Breval's *The Play is the Plot* (1718), Sandford's *The Female Fop; Or, The False One Fitted* (1723), and Gabriel Odingsells' *The Capricious Lovers* (1725). The depiction of the local scene provides the chief resource of these plays. All are undistinguished, and only Breval's farce need concern us here. In Sir Barnaby Bindover, Breval presents an interesting variant on the conventional avaricious old father who plans to marry his daughter against her wishes to a rich man. Sir Barnaby has apparently become a country squire only after making a fortune as a merchant—as he explains in the soliloquy that opens the play. "He is discover'd by himself, looking over his Accounts; he shuts his Books, knocks out his Pipe, and comes forward."

SIR BARNABY BINDOVER: So much for this;—Fortune I thank thee;—had my Father sent me to a College, when he plac'd me behind a Compter, I had been (twenty to one) some Country, Humdrum, Ale-guzling Vicar, with a fourscore Pound Income, some fifty Doses of Opium for my Parishioners, ten Children, and as many Tithe Pigs.—My good Genius put it into the old Gentleman's Head to bind me out Apprentice, and I am now Sir *Barnaby Bindover*, Knight-Batchelour, and Justice of the *Quorum* for the County of *Bedford*, with two thousand Pounds *per Annum* and twenty thousand in my Pocket. Then I have bury'd my Wife, and have but one Daughter to provide for; in good faith no bad Circumstance—

The self-satisfaction apparent here marks the speaker as an appropriate butt of the pranks to come later: he is made to appear a fool and is tricked by his daughter and the young man she loves. But the pranks are stale and the plot staler; it is the rural scene that makes the farce lively. Treated neither sentimentally nor satirically, the Bedfordshire village with its rustic inhabitants provides variety and vigor in a farce that would seem only too commonplace if it had a London setting. Sir Barnaby is unusual solely because of his status: to my knowledge, this is the only play of George I's reign that introduces as a principal character a rich merchant turned country squire. In actual life, the transition from merchant to squire was at this time made frequently.[25]

Apart from these comedies of country locales, comedies with settings in London continued to include characters who, even if at the moment in town, had rusticity strong upon them. If there had long been recognition of the oversimplification embodied in the booby-squire stereotype, there was as yet no sustained reaction from it.

FIVE

The Displacement of the Restoration Tradition, 1728-1737

Just as the political debates preliminary to the Treaty of Utrecht brought an important modification in comedy, so also did the more acrimonious debates occasioned by Walpole's prolonged tenure of office.

As the futility of the Jacobite cause became steadily more clear in the 1720's,[1] the political attention of the dramatists turned increasingly to the antagonism between the Walpole government and the opposition—the coalition of disaffected Whigs and Tories of which William Pulteney became the leader. When George II after his accession in 1727 confirmed Walpole in authority, the clamor against the Great Man reached a sustained loudness, and less than a year later—with *The Beggar's Opera* in 1728—it began to be heard in the drama.

Comedy of the decade after 1728 differs from the earlier comedy notably in its heavy burden of complaint about the alleged political, social, and intellectual degeneration of England. Whereas the earlier plays are socially and politically complacent, those of Gay, Fielding, and others are aggressively critical, like the satires of Swift and Pope—*Gulliver's Travels*, the *Epistles to Several Persons*, and the *Imitations of Horace*—to which they provide a dramatic parallel. Their belaboring of the alleged corruption of the Walpole government ultimately became intolerable to Walpole, who replied to it with the Licensing Act of 1737.[2]

Since the last years of the seventeenth century benevolistic ethical theory had often inhibited the satirical treatment of manners characteristic of Restoration comedy,[3] yet through most of the first three decades of the eighteenth century, as we have seen, comedies abound with stock characters and plot relationships that were inherited from the earlier period. If from the beginning of the century modifications in the social and moral assumptions of comedy appear, still character-types and plots remain fairly constant through the middle 1720's, roughly until *The Beggar's Opera* (1728). Thereafter, comedies are frequently written (by Henry Fielding, Robert Dodsley, and James Miller, among others, in addition to Gay) that depart radically from the older pattern of the love chase, often including social commentary rather than love intrigue as their chief resource. The change in the general tenor of comedy came rather sharply in 1728. The stock character of the merchant, for example, the stereotype most clearly embodying a social judgment, occurs in only a few instances between 1728 and 1737. Apart from James Miller's *The Man of Taste* (1735), the character is present in fully developed form only in the most trivial of farces and ballad operas.

A new era in theatrical affairs began about the same time. The number of theaters regularly operating in London rose from two to five in about four years.[4] Drury Lane had presented plays steadily since the Restoration, and Lincoln's Inn Fields since 1714. The two theaters in the Haymarket, the "Opera House" (opened in 1705) and the "Little Theatre" (opened in 1720), were in their earlier years used only intermittently—the opera house, then and later, mainly for music. Beginning in 1728, however, the Little Theatre in the Haymarket, operating under a series of managers (among them Fielding), became an active force in theatrical affairs, notable for some audacious dramatic experiments. In 1729 Goodman's Fields Theatre was opened in East London, and it remained open until the 1740's. In 1732 John Rich transferred his company from Lincoln's Inn Fields to his handsome new theater in Covent Garden, which thereafter shared theatrical supremacy with Drury Lane; but the Lincoln's Inn Fields Theatre continued to be used by other companies until 1737.

The actor-managers of Drury Lane—Barton Booth, Robert Wilks, and Colley Cibber—dominant figures in the theater of George I's time, reached the end of their long collective management of Drury Lane in the early 1730's: Wilks died in 1732 and Booth in 1733, and Cibber withdrew from the management in 1733. They were succeeded by John Highmore, and, after a short interval, by Charles Fleetwood; neither had extensive knowledge of the theater before becoming manager, and neither had much success. John Rich remained an influential figure in the London theaters, at Lincoln's Inn Fields until 1732 and thereafter at Covent Garden. Insensitive to the literary qualities of drama from the beginning of his career, he was encouraged by the huge financial success of *The Beggar's Opera* to concentrate on musical and pantomimic experiments at the expense of traditional comedy and tragedy. Indeed nearly all of the London theatrical managers of the 1730's did the same.

At no time in the early 1700's were the theaters without articulate critics and internal dissensions; but the expressions of dissatisfaction within and without the theaters seem to have grown more shrill in the 1730's. The actor-managers of Drury Lane, for all the criticism they had attracted, were thoroughly competent professionals who had provided a stabilizing force in the theaters that was missed after their time.

The society that is the ostensible subject of *The Beggar's Opera* is intensely urban, corrupt in a way peculiar to large cities. Gay, and the many opposition satirists who followed him in the decade after 1728, found in London life (then in the gin age depicted so frighteningly in Hogarth's prints) a type of the corruption that they alleged to be overtaking the nation. They professed to see in the contrast between rural and urban life a contrast between an old and vigorous way of English life that had made England strong and a new and debauched way that threatened destruction. Along with harsh treatments of London, they introduced into more and more plays an idealized version of the country.

To be sure, the rusticity of some of the plays is a mere matter of the pastoralism of literary convention. The locale of Colley Cibber's *Love in a Riddle* (1729), for example, is *"the Arcadian Fields,"* a locale retained in the shortened version, *Damon and Phillida* (1729). Cibber's characters have classical names, and his conception of them and their capers owes much to convention. The rusticity, too, of Allan Ramsay's *The Gentle Shepherd* is colored by pastoral tradition, though the rusticity is far more convincing and far more pleasing than that in Cibber's plays. Not originally intended for the stage, *The Gentle Shepherd*, first published in 1725, was reworked in ballad opera form after the success of *The Beggar's Opera*, and was performed often in Scotland. It was performed in London in 1730 in a shortened adaptation by Theophilus Cibber under a different title, *Patie and Peggie*.[5] That a professional like Theophilus Cibber should choose Ramsay's play as the subject of an adaptation—a pastoral play with Scotch characters and with a setting in the Scotch countryside—tells much about the taste of London audiences for plays of country life.

A taste for the pastoral had been alive in England since the Renaissance; in this sense the new vogue of rusticity was no innovation. Many of the dramatists' encomiums on rural life are mere echoes of literary commonplaces that derive from classical antiquity.[6] Many others, however, derive largely or wholly from a widely felt concern about the increasingly appalling condition of life in London.

I shall consider Robert Dodsley's plays at length below. Here it is enough to note that in his *The King and the Miller of Mansfield* (1737), *Sir John Cockle at Court* (1738), and *The Blind Beggar of Bethnel Green* (1741), the central character is an admirable countryman—in the first two, the same man, John Cockle. In *The King and the Miller* Cockle's son talks about London, from which he has just returned, in such critical terms that the father congratulates himself on living in the country; and in the sequel his own experiences in London confirm him in his prejudice against urban life. The countrymen in Dodsley's plays exemplify austerity in opposition to the luxury that breeds corruption. On a typical note Cockle in *Sir John Cockle at Court* offers advice to his king, on the subject of courtiers, in a recommendation of austerity—which includes a surreptitious hit at Walpole (Sc. 2):

The Man whom a King employs, or a Nation trusts, should first be thoroughly try'd. Examine his private Character; mark how he lives; is he luxurious, or proud, or ambitious, or extravagant; avoid him: The Soul of that Man is mean: Necessity will press him, and publick Fraud must pay his private Debts.

Rusticity in a moralistic mood is present in George Lillo's first play, *Silvia; Or, The Country Burial* (1730), a ballad opera. The earnestness of *George Barnwell* is foreshadowed in Lillo's treatment of a situation that became hackneyed in later melodrama: a landowner's attempt, here unsuccessful, to seduce the virtuous daughter of a poor man. The landowner's libertinism gives rise to certain reflections, and Lillo is at pains to assert the claims of humble people to respectful consideration. The earnestness is by no means sustained, however. Lillo resolves the dramatic action by the conventional device of revealing previously unknown family relationships that show the landowner and the poor man's daughter to be social equals and thus appropriate partners for marriage; moreover, he includes a farcical subplot on the theme of the subtitle.

A number of comedies, farces, and ballad operas of the 1730's exploit rustic customs as well as characters. John Hippisley's *Flora* (1729) and *A Sequel to the Opera of Flora* (1732), Essex Hawker's *The Wedding; . . . With an Hudibrastic Skimmington* (1729), Charles Coffee's *Southwark Fair; Or, The Sheep Shearing* (1729), and Edward Phillips' *The Livery Rake and Country Lass* (1733), among others, show playwrights experimenting, most often in broad farce, with rural themes. If these pieces do not exactly idealize country life, they all exhibit high relish for the countryside, a relish that was rare indeed thirty years earlier.

Rusticity reaches an extreme in Joseph Dorman's *Sir Roger de Coverley; Or, The Merry Christmas* (1740), a sentimental rendering of life at the manor house of Addison's and Steele's famous character. Lacking action, the entertainment is remarkable chiefly for its idealized picture of the holiday in the country, a picture not different in essentials from that produced by Washington Irving nearly a century later. Entering "A large Country-Hall stuck with Holly and Bays," Sir Roger instructs his housekeeper (I):

SIR ROGER: Be sure, *Prudence,* you take care to let us have Plenty today.—Beef, Pudding, Plumb-Porridge, and Mince-Pies in Abundance.—My honest Neighbours love them; and today's⸍ the Day they make me happy.

PRUDENCE: The Day your Honour makes them so, rather, Sir.

SIR ROGER: That's what I mean, Prudence. The making them happy makes me so too. I'm always delighted at the Felicity of others; but more especially, if I my self have been the Cause on't.

The character of Sir Roger, it will be apparent, was conceived under the influence of benevolistic theories; and typical of the literature of the times, he appears as a countryman.

Along with these plays of rustic life, as we have seen, appeared other plays that are intensely urban in the specialized way of *The Beggar's Opera*—that is, they are taken up with the life of London's underworld.[7] The charm of humble life in the country, and the horror of humble life in London: these are twin themes of the drama in the years after Gay (whether or not he was motivated by Swift's suggestion that he write a Newgate pastoral) demonstrated the dramatic possibilities of low life. To be sure, *The Beggar's Opera* and the imitations of it treat low life humorously, sometimes even tenderly; the dramatists sought in the lives of jailbirds and prostitutes the same kind of novelty, of colorful detail, that they sought in rustic life. But the humor of the underworld has a grotesque aspect that is foreign to the humor of the countryside. The parallel of Hogarth's narrative prints has often been invoked, with good reason, to suggest the special kind of grotesque humor conveyed in the farces and ballad operas of the decade after *The Beggar's Opera*. Christopher Bullock's early *Woman's Revenge; Or, A Match in Newgate* (1715), the anonymous *The Lottery* (1728; not Fielding's play of the same name), Charles Coffee's *The Beggar's Wedding* (1729; this time the urban setting is provided by Dublin), Fielding's *The Covent-Garden Tragedy* (1732), and the anonymous and allegorical *The Deposing and Death of Queen Gin* (1736) are but a few of the plays which in various forms portray urban corruption. Although the term "town pastoral" is useful in suggesting the literary ancestry of these plays, the term must not be allowed to obscure a difference in tone between them and the dramatic "pastorals" with rural settings.

Gay's *Polly* (1729), the celebrated sequel to *The Beggar's Opera* which was refused licensing for stage production by the Lord Chamberlain, provides in a single play a contrast between urban corruption and primitive innocence: between a group of transported felons, warped by an early life in London, and a group of Indians, whose nobility bears witness to an early life passed in isolation from the corruptions of society. The locale of the play is the West Indies: it is one of the few English plays of the early eighteenth century with an American setting. In the establishment of the bawd Trapes, the scene of the earlier part of the action, Gay portrays a brothel apparently intended to be comically similar to such establishments in London; and he turns the colonists' emulation of the sins of Londoners to comic advantage. In *Polly* as in *The Beggar's Opera*, he implies a similarity between corruption in low life and that in high life, using the similarity as a vehicle for political satire. "I wonder I am not more wealthy," observes Trapes (I),

for, o' my conscience, I have as few scruples as those that are ten thousand times as rich. But, alack-a-day! I am forc'd to play at small game. I now and then betray and ruine an innocent girl. . . . Can I in conscience expect to be equally rich with those who betray and ruine provinces and countries?

The Indians, by contrast, are portrayed as noble savages. The Indian king, whose perplexed queries about European civilization resemble those of eighteenth-century literary "citizens of the world," is a completely rational man. A conversation (III) between him and Morano, who is Macheath in blackface disguise, may well have been suggested by the conversation between Gulliver and the king of Brobdingnag in *Gulliver's Travels*:

POHETOHEE [the king]: Would your *European* laws have suffer'd crimes like these [acts of piracy] to have gone unpunish'd!
MORANO: Were all I am worth safely landed, I have wherewithal to make almost any crime sit easy upon me.
POHETOHEE: Have ye notions of property?
MORANO: Of my own.
POHETOHEE: Would not your honest industry have been sufficient to have supported you?
MORANO: Honest industry! I have heard talk of it indeed among the people, but all great genius's are above it.
POHETOHEE: Have you no respect for virtue?
MORANO: As a good phrase, Sir. But the practicers of it are so insignificant and poor, that they are seldom found in the best company.
POHETOHEE: Is not wisdom esteem'd among you?
MORANO: Yes, Sir: But only as a step to riches and power; a step that raises ourselves, and trips up our neighbors.
POHETOHEE: Honour, and honesty, are not those distinguish'd?
MORANO: As incapacities and follies. How ignorant are these *Indians!* But indeed I think honour is of some use; it serves to swear upon.
POHETOHEE: Have you no consciousness? Have you no shame?

MORANO: Of being poor.
POHETOHEE: How can society subsist with avarice! Ye are but the
forms of men. Beasts would thrust you out of their herd upon
that account, and man should cast you out for your brutal dis-
positions.

The Indian king's concluding judgment, it will be noted, is not
far from the Brobdingnagian king's conclusion that Europeans
are a race of "little odious Vermin."

The contrast established in *Polly* between virtuous and corrupt characters is, of course, lacking in *The Beggar's Opera*, in
which all the characters, even to some extent the two attractive
heroines, share the moral assumptions of their underworld
society. In this difference between the two plays lies one reason
for the superiority of *The Beggar's Opera*: it has a unity of tone
lacking in *Polly*, in which the moral abandon of the depraved
characters cannot be relished because it is necessarily viewed
through the censorious eyes of the rational Indians. We are
compelled in *Polly* to take on the attitudes of the Indians,
rational attitudes, and having done so we are too censorious of
the colonists and pirates to enjoy their misdeeds. In other
words, the presence of the two societies in *Polly* makes impossible the insouciant tone that is the special merit of the earlier
play.

Because dramatists in the late seventeenth and earlier eighteenth centuries were indifferent to ideas with bold implications
in political thory, it is easy to overestimate the originality of
dramatists after 1728 in exploring social questions. Scarcely
any English comedy in the thirty-five years before the appearance of *The Beggar's Opera* contained a hint that the hierarchical order of English society—with its immense and, to the
twentieth-century mind, shocking inequalities of wealth, privilege, and opportunity—was not an inalienable condition of life.
The tradition of genteel comedy deriving from the Restoration,
with its focus on the narrow spectrum of society in which the
gentry and the nobility mingled, perpetuated the social assumptions of the group that provided its subject, a conservative group that had nothing to gain by change. Not until the
1730's did dramatists generally acknowledge the merchants'
claim to social consideration, and even then most of the drama-

tists gave no evidence of discarding their assumption of the rightness of a hierarchical social order: they merely acknowledged wealth and mercantile prominence as entitlements to high place.

In *The Beggar's Opera* there is a hint, perhaps on Gay's part an unintentional hint, of bolder views.[8] Gay's nominal subject is, of course, low life. The effectiveness of the play depends on the distance he establishes between the moral and social orders of the dramatic action and those of the lives of his contemporaries. The characters live with indifference to conventional moral and social discriminations, an indifference that could force the audience to consider what was usually taken for granted. Gay's beggars, observing irrationalities in English customs with an incredulous detachment, serve a literary function analogous to that of the eighteenth-century imaginary travelers: Montesquieu's Persian gentleman, Swift's Gulliver, Voltaire's Micromégas, and Goldsmith's Chinese gentleman, among others. The beggars, like the travelers, have the emotional detachment of outsiders and the resultant perspicacity; and they have, also like the travelers, the privilege of uninhibited comment granted to those who are totally uncommitted to the society that provides their subject.

We should be more inclined to see bold social comment in *The Beggar's Opera* had the subsequent history of England produced a revolution. Our view of history, conditioned by the analogy of organic evolution, leads us to evaluate earlier events—including such literary events as *The Beggar's Opera* —with reference to what happened later. England, unlike France, maintained its hierarchical, aristocratic structure throughout the eighteenth century. Consequently, we are led to emphasize eighteenth-century French social protests appearing in imaginative literature and to overlook parallel English instances. Certainly French literature of social criticism was more sustained, more eloquent, and more forthright than the English, just as it was more effective in producing action. Still, the continuing English conservatism leads us to underestimate the intensity of the protest against social inequalities by such writers as Gay, Fielding, and Dodsley.

Gay in *The Beggar's Opera* submits class relationships to scrutiny through the device of inverting them: the lowest class, that of the highwaymen and beggars, is assumed to be of more consequence than the highest, that of the gentlemen and peers who govern the nation. This simple inversion, maintained without falter, carries the burden of Gay's social critique, which is not the less effective for its simplicity. No elaborate argument was needed to make the point that men, whatever their station, are fundamentally alike: that accidents of birth and fortune, more than differences in virtue and abilities, accounted for the immense discrepancies of privilege in the eighteenth century. The bare structure of *The Beggar's Opera* had subversive implications—and it was indeed deemed to be subversive by some eighteenth-century critics.[9]

It was the immense popularity of *The Beggar's Opera* that made it a strong dramatic and political force; and its popularity was a consequence of a fusion of topical and more generalized satire, all of it assimilated in a deftly turned musical play. Not a political allegory, *The Beggar's Opera* nevertheless conveys sustained criticism of Walpole, who is variously suggested in the characters of Macheath the highwayman, Peachum the "screen," and Robin of Bagshot, one of the lesser thieves. All of these characters move in a mock-heroic world (by implication the world of Walpole's government) in which peculation, bribery, and treachery are conditions of life. The fusion of topical denunciation with generalized social criticism gives intensity to the whole. Where, in other writers, the topical and the generalized are not joined, the former often seems trivial and the latter effete.

The Beggar's Opera was the most imitated of early-eighteenth-century plays, giving rise in fact to a group of ballad operas that forms a distinct sub-genre.[10] None of these plays, not even the later ones written by Gay himself, rival in quality *The Beggar's Opera*; but many are competent, and a few include interesting social comment.

Robert Dodsley's plays, despite their mediocrity, merit attention in this context. His first four plays were afterpieces, dramatic entertainments that structurally and ideologically represent experiments (the last two in ballad opera form). In each of the four appears as a central figure an old man, of strong character himself, who passes his time in loquacious discussion of the meanness and irrationality of his fellow men. This central character approximates a dramatization of the eccentric commentator of the periodical essays—Isaac Bickerstaff and Nestor Ironside, among a host of others—but his views are bolder than those of the periodical commentator, and, if moralistic in bias, they have a closer applicability to social relationships.

Dodsley's best afterpiece, *The King and the Miller of Mansfield* (1737), may owe something of its force to suggestions taken, directly or indirectly, from Lope de Vega's *El Mejor Alcalde, el Rey*.[11] Dodsley contrives to give his miller freedom of speech before his king (one of the Henrys) by bringing them together in a forest, the miller not recognizing the king, who has been separated from his retainers while hunting. Pleased with the miller's manly independence and originality of thought and speech, the king goes with him to his cottage nearby and is entertained incognito. Meanwhile, the miller's son returns home a fugitive, the victim of unjust accusations made by a nobleman who has seduced his sweetheart. Subsequently, the king, acting as dispenser of justice, repairs the wrongs done to the miller's son and his sweetheart and punishes the nobleman.

Dodsley's dramatic action, it will appear, is such as to emphasize the inherent equality of men. When the king and the miller meet on equal terms in the forest, the miller perceives no superior qualities in the unknown stranger. The king himself, before he encounters the miller, muses on his helplessness when he is separated from his companions (p. 11): "Of what Advantage is it now to be a King? Night shews me no Respect: I cannot see better, nor walk so well, as another Man. What is a King? Is he wiser than another Man?" The contrast that subsequently emerges between the miller and the aristocrats who are the king's retainers turns altogether in the miller's favor; and the act of villany that the king sets right is itself an instance of the abuse of aristocratic privilege. The play, for all its gentle and sentimental surface, differs altogether in its social assumptions from the genteel comedies that had been the dramatic staple.

The egalitarian theme is not necessarily a reflection of eighteenth-century political thought. Lope de Vega and other Spanish Renaissance dramatists often take as a subject an aristocrat's act of oppression, and frequently they use the king as a symbol of justice, an agent who restores a proper relationship between social classes; moreover, they insist on the dignity of the individual of whatever station. English Renaissance dramatists, too, sometimes assert the claims to respect of humble folk—in *The Shoemaker's Holiday*, for example—though much less often than the Spaniards. These background considerations are relevant in posing this question: is *The King and the Miller* a mere rehandling of a Renaissance theme or an early expression of eighteenth-century egalitarianism—or both?

It is both, I think. It seems clear that Dodsley was attracted to the subject of the play by its egalitarian implications; for one thing, his other early plays strike the same note. Dodsley's sympathies are indeed consistently with the humble, and with the virtues of integrity and independence, which to him they represent—as suggested succinctly in the following exchange in *The King and the Miller* (p. 31):

THE MILLER [upon hearing his son's strongly critical account of London]: Well, if this is *London,* give me my Country Cottage; which, tho' it is not a great House, nor a fine House, is my own House, and I can shew a Receipt for the Building on't.
THE KING: I wish all the great Builders in the Kingdom could say as much.

This assertion of the merit of humble persons is distinct from the Renaissance insistence that persons of every rank are entitled to respect so long as they fulfill the obligations of their rank. Conversely, there is no overt insistence on the rightness of the hierarchical structure of society as there is in *El Mejor Alcalde*; no insistence, that is, that the subordination of the humble is a necessary condition of the health of society. There is no glorification, say, of the idea of kingship, though the king is respectfully portrayed as an administrator of justice, and there are no sympathetic portrayals of aristocrats in their appropriate dignity.

Dodsley's afterpieces—*The Toy Shop, The King and the Miller, Sir John Cockle at Court,* and *The Blind Beggar of Bethnal Green*—for all their sententiousness, came closer than any earlier eighteenth-century plays to asserting that rank and wealth are unimportant determinants of a man's worth. (Significantly, Dodsley had been a footman before he turned to writing plays.) Certainly there is no hint that he advocated revolutionary action, or that anyone who saw his plays thought that he advocated it; but he brought a more audacious set of assumptions to the drama than had his immediate predecessors.

James Miller, conservative enough in most of his plays, includes in his *Art and Nature* (1738) a foreigner, a "citizen of the world" who functions as a rationalistic and uninhibited commentator on English life. Miller took the conception for this character, as for the play as a whole, from French sources[12] —a fact that presumably explains the marked differences between this and his other plays. The foreign commentator is an American Indian, a man of "pure natural Wit, strong good Sense and Integrity of Soul" (I), who is amazed by the irrationalities of English life. Truemore, the young gentleman who has brought him to England, instructs him (III):

TRUEMORE: There are among us two sorts of People, the Rich and the Poor; the Rich have all the Money, and the Poor none.

JULIO: A very equal Distribution truly.

TRUEMORE: They are under a Necessity of working for the Rich, who give them Money in proportion to their Labour.

JULIO: And pray, what do the Rich do, whilst the Poor work for 'em?

TRUEMORE: Eat, Drink, Sleep, and Dress, and pass their whole time in Diversions and Entertainments.

JULIO: This indeed is very happy for the Rich.

TRUEMORE: The happiness which you imagine in their Condition, is very often the Cause of their Misery.

JULIO: Hey? How so?

TRUEMORE: Because Riches only multiply Mens Cares; the Poor labour only for the Necessaries, but the Rich for the Superfluities of Life; which are boundless by reason of their Ambition, Luxury, and Vanity which consume them; thus the rich Man's Wealth is the Cause of his Labour and Want.[18]

The distance between the dramatic exposition of such views and actual revolutionary doctrine, it will appear, is not great. Even so, that distance was not traversed in the early eighteenth century.

In John Kelly's *Timon in Love; Or, The Innocent Theft*

(1733), an adaptation of a play by de L'Isle,[14] we once again find mythological characters in implausible situations speaking good sense about political matters—above all, about the power of gold to corrupt. The denunciation of corruption implicit in the play was no doubt intended as a hit at Walpole (Kelly wrote a later play, openly political, that was forbidden by the Lord Chamberlain),[15] but the satire is generalized. The simple dramatic action serves to elicit conversations that are the play's chief resource. Timon, a misanthropic recluse, obtains the favor of Jupiter, who gives him money and grants his wish that his ass be made capable of speech; and in the ensuing conversations he and his ass show most interest in the use of wealth. The play has clear thematic affinities with the major contemporary nondramatic satires, revealing, as do those greater works, certainly not a revolutionary restiveness but a deep conviction, compatible with social conservatism, that England has fallen prey to a consuming and enervating avarice.

Henry Fielding's comedies, farces, burlesques, and ballad operas, in their forms and in their themes, provide an epitome of the dramatic activity from 1728 to 1737. With a facility rarely surpassed in England, he produced twenty-odd plays in the nine-year span, some of them brief and inconsiderable farces obviously turned out in the short pauses of an active career, but others memorable dramatic expressions of the age. He was intensely in touch with his times: the contemporaneity of his plays is at once their merit and their limitation, the source of their vigor and their value as records of London life in the age of Walpole, Pope, and Hogarth, but the source also of the barrier to intelligibility that now limits the number of their readers to special students of the age. Fielding followed contemporary theatrical fashions and at the same time modified them: he wrote, but with a difference, comedies of fashionable life in the manner of Congreve; political and theatrical burlesques, some of them in the ballad opera form popularized by Gay; and farces, some in the native tradition and some in the French.[16] Like nearly every other important writer of the 1730's he was caught up in the political debates; and like most of his fellow dramatists he wrote plays with political overtones. Finally, of course, his dramatic forays into politics terminated his career in the theater. He is the single most important figure in the theater of the 1730's, but rather because of his cumulative achievement than because of high achievement in particular plays.

On the social issues that concern us here, his attitudes are curiously ambivalent. As we have seen, he used the dunciad theme, in *The Author's Farce* (1730 and 1734) and in *Pasquin* (1736), with its implied conservative judgment on social and literary change. He takes the commercialization of literature as his satirical mark in *The Author's Farce*; and he devotes one of the two "stage rehearsals" in *Pasquin* to an allegorical lament for England's commercial society, in which (V)

> Cits shall turn Beaus, and taste *Italian* Songs,
> While Courtiers are Stock-jobbing in the City.

In all of his plays he is censorious of the contemporary preoccupation with money, which other writers attributed to the rise in prominence of the business community. He repeatedly satirizes mercenary attitudes toward marriage—as in *Love in Several Masques* (1728) and *Don Quixote in England* (1734). "Money is a Thing well worth considering in these Affairs," observes Don Quixote, with such good sense that he obviously speaks for the author (III), "but Parents always regard it too much and Lovers too little. No Match can be happy which Love and Fortune do not conspire to make so." He is critical, too, of the current preoccupation with stockjobbing. Sir Avarice Pedant in *The Temple Beau* (1730), whose antecedents are country gentlemen rather than merchants, exhibits in his constricted personality the results of overmuch concern with trading in stocks. His views ironically convey Fielding's (V):

Learning is a fine thing indeed, in an Age when of the few that have it, the greater Part starve. I remember when a Set of strange Fellows us'd to meet at *Wills* Coffee-House; but now it's another *Change-Alley*. Every Man now who wou'd live, must be a Stock-Jobber.

Yet his aversion to money-mindedness notwithstanding, Fielding did not satirize the merchants. On the contrary, he praises them in *The Champion* and *The Journal of a Voyage to Lisbon*, and in his novel *Jonathan Wild* he portrays a most admirable merchant in Heartfree; moreover, he supported Lillo's experiments in merchant-class tragedy. His closest approach to the stereotype appears in Mr. Wisdom of the farce *The Letter Writers; Or, A New Way to Keep a Wife at Home* (1731), a conventional piece about a merchant with a flirtatious wife; but he gives little attention to the character's occupation. In *The Intriguing Chambermaid* (1734) he depicts respectfully the merchant father of the young gentleman who is the chief character; and he scores some bitter hits at the social presumption of lords. He praises the merchants convincingly in *The Author's Farce* through a normative character, Witmore (I); and in *Pasquin* (1736) he includes ironic comment on the aristocratic disdain for commerce (III). In brief, he had a healthy respect for the business community even while he regretted some of the results of its growth.

The central social antithesis of his plays as of his novels is not that between merchants and gentlemen, but that between residents in rural and in urban England. In all his novels— *Joseph Andrews, Jonathan Wild, Tom Jones,* and *Amelia*— London life is depicted as corrupt; in all except *Jonathan Wild* the sympathetic characters are finally rewarded with retirement to the country; in all again except *Jonathan Wild* the conspicuously benevolent characters are residents of the country whereas most, though not all, of the depraved characters are Londoners. Sometimes, like other opposition writers, he used the corruption of London as a symbol of the corruption of Walpole's government; in *Jonathan Wild* most explicitly, but also in *The Covent Garden Tragedy*. Fashionable London appears in the third part of *Tom Jones* and in *Amelia* as chilling in its depravity.

So also in the plays. In *Love in Several Masques* and *The Temple Beau,* and to a more marked degree in *The Modern Husband, The Universal Gallant,* and *The Wedding Day* (all comedies of fashionable London), Fielding depicts the ugliness of a rich, sophisticated, but degenerate *beau monde*. In *The Modern Husband,* to take the most extreme example, the man who gives the play its name lives by discreetly selling his wife's favors; and the purchaser who is represented most harshly is the single lord of the play, an abandoned sensualist possessing

none of the redeeming wit of Etherege's and Congreve's liber-
tines. Parallel with the plays portraying the corruption of
fashionable life are several presenting a harsh view of London low life: *The Lottery, The Covent-Garden Tragedy*, and
Miss Lucy in Town. Fielding's hostile judgment of London,
then, was comprehensive and unambiguous.

His five-act comedies published or produced before 1737
are *Love in Several Masques* (1728), *The Temple Beau*
(1730), *Rape upon Rape; Or, The Justice Caught in His Own
Trap* (1730), *The Modern Husband* (1732), and *The Universal Gallant; Or, The Different Husbands* (1735). All but
Rape upon Rape, with its broadly farcical conception of characters and action, show a certain homogeneity. With the one
exception, they portray characters of fashionable life. It is in
them we may find Fielding's variations on the conventions of
Restoration comedy.

Love in Several Masques and *The Temple Beau* focus on
the love intrigues, including conventional guardian outwittings,
of young couples who wish to be married; whereas *The Modern Husband* and *The Universal Gallant* focus on the illicit
love intrigues of couples already married (though there is
subordinate attention to licit courtships). An important difference in tone results: the two later plays are far more bitter than
the earlier. Yet one theme runs through all (except perhaps
The Universal Gallant): a sense of outrage at the subordination, actual or attempted, of love to money in marriage. "Let
meaner Things be bought and sold," so goes the concluding,
and thematic, song in *Love in Several Masques*, "But Beauty
never truck'd for Gold."

Love in Several Masques and *The Temple Beau* are conventional and competent, if quite undistinguished, comedies in
the manner of Congreve (in their plotting, their attempted
epigram, their satirical review of manners, and their characters)
but with some notable differences in social values. Most conspicuously, Congreve's strong implied endorsement of prudence in financial affairs is absent here. In Congreve, the sympathetic characters conduct their love affairs with close attention to property settlements; in Fielding, by contrast, they
protest the entanglement of mercenary considerations with

marriage. Thus the following exchange in *Love in Several Masques* (II):

HELENA: To be sold! to be put up at Auction! to be disposed of, as a piece of Goods, by way of Bargain and Sale.

LADY TRAP: Niece, Niece, you are dealt with, as a piece of rich Goods; you are disposed of at a high Price; Sir *Positive* understands the World, and will make good Conditions for you.

The sympathetic characters in *The Temple Beau* act with a disinterestedness quite like Helena's, whereas the satirical characters, notably Sir Avarice Pedant, are even more mercenary than her aunt.

In *Love in Several Masques* Fielding chooses as the subject of his strongest satire the affectations of the wellborn— notably their family pride. In doing so he dramatizes, more explicitly than any of his contemporaries, one of the most important hostilities created by the agricultural economy of the eighteenth century: that between the baronets and the lords, or, more precisely, between the lesser landowners, who as a group were becoming poorer, and the greater landowners, who as a group were becoming richer.[17] In view of the amount of attention lavished on other social rivalries, it is curious that so little was expended on this one. The urban bias of comedy presumably accounts for the omission. Sir Positive Trap and Lord Formal of *Love in Several Masques* are both satirically conceived representatives of their respective stations (III):

LORD FORMAL: Pray, Sir, who are the *Traps?*

SIR POSITIVE TRAP: Why, Sir, the *Traps* are a venerable Family. We have had, at least, fifty Knights of the Shire, Deputy-Lieutenants, and Colonels of the Militia in it. Perhaps the Grand-Mogul has not a nobler Coat of Arms. It is, Sir, a Lion Rampant, with a Wolf Couchant, and a Cat Currant, in a Field Gules.

LORD FORMAL: It wants nothing but Supporters to be very noble, truly.

SIR POSITIVE TRAP: Supporters, Sir! It has Six thousand a Year to support its Nobility, and Six thousand Years to support its Antiquity.

LORD FORMAL: You will give me Leave to presume, Sir, with all the Deference imaginable to your Superiority of Judgment, to doubt whether it be practicable to confer the Title of Noble on

any Coat of Arms that labours under the deplorable deficiency
of a coronet.

. . .

SIR POSITIVE TRAP: He is a Lord then, and what of that! An old
English Baronet is above a Lord. A Title of Yesterday! an
Innovation! Who were Lords, I wonder, in the Time of
Sir *Julius Caesar?* And, it is plain, he was a Baronet, by his
being called by his Christian Name.

Baronets and lords are Fielding's fools.

If in *Love in Several Masques* and *The Temple Beau*
Fielding introduces variations in the formalized pattern of
comedy deriving from the Restoration, in *The Modern Husband* he breaks abruptly with that pattern. In this comedy,
which bears a resemblance to his novel *Amelia*, there is a departure from the customary stylization in character types, plotting, and dialogue sufficiently pronounced as to come as a jolt
to readers long familiar with the plays of the earlier dramatists. All at once we seem to be entering the domain of the
novel, so completely has stylization given way to natural dialogue and the gay love chase to the analysis of character, motive , and environment. The play was not popular with its first
audiences, nor has it been with subsequent critics, one of whom
calls it "one of the dullest productions ever fathered by a man
of genius."[18] Serious overstatement, I think, but an under-
standable judgment of a critic whose taste was formed on the
best of Restoration comedy, for the play has none of the
Restoration's distinctive excellencies and few of its distinctive
qualities. The play has, to be sure, a concentration on sexual
relations, as have the earlier ones, but even this in an altogether
different spirit. There is no gaiety in sex in *The Modern Husband*, no witty transformation of animal attraction into an
intellectual game; rather, sex remains an awkward fact of life,
like poverty, which is a degrading and corrupting force. Fielding the embittered analyst of the personality and of society is
too much in evidence here for the play to have the merits traditional to comedy.

The sex intrigue of the play is largely motivated, on one
side at least, by money. As we have seen, Mr. Modern, the title
character, pimps for his wife. Having lost a fortune in the

South Sea and other financial adventures, he and his wife never-theless desperately maintain the appearance of fashion, by bor-rowing and gambling as well as by discreet prostitution. The railing review of the town in their conversation and in that of others would suggest that such a mode of life was far from uncommon. Lord Richly, formerly a paying lover of Mrs. Modern, in attempting to seduce another married woman (Mrs. Bellamant, an earlier version of the faithful Amelia of the novel), exclaims to her when she repulses him (IV): "How many Families are supported by this Method which you start at? Does not many a Woman in this Town drive her Hus-band's Coach?" So at any rate Fielding would suggest in this play. The social attitudes of the Restoration are replaced here by those of Walpole's England.

The Universal Gallant is in subject and tone a companion piece to *The Modern Husband*, though it has fewer of the novelistic qualities. Like the earlier play it conveys an im-pression of debauchery in fashionable life that is not softened by a surface wit: its subject, emphasized in intrigue and con-versation alike, is marital infidelity in a corrupt London.

Fielding's corollary to London is, of course, the uncor-rupted countryside, mentioned often even in the comedies of high life as a refuge for virtue. His most attractive dramatic portrayal of country life appears in *Don Quixote in England*, which in its locale, its tone, and its indebtedness to Cervantes has a special relationship to *Joseph Andrews*. *Don Quixote in England* is a sharply satirical play, a withering review of the machinery by which elections were bought. It is Squire Badger, however, an earlier Squire Western, who with his fox-hunting songs and good spirits establishes the tone of the comedy, which is altogether English and conservative.

Satire notwithstanding, then, Fielding's writings reveal a certain conservatism,[19] notably in their rather strict observation of the traditional relationships between classes. Yet he has an eye to the irony of social distinctions, the huge disparity often existing between rank and natural merit; and in at least two of his farces he expresses ideas that can bear an egalitarian inter-pretation—*An Old Man Taught Wisdom; Or, The Virgin Unmasked* (1735) and *Miss Lucy in Town, A Sequel to the Virgin Unmasked* (1742). In the earlier farce there is perhaps the nearest approach in early-eighteenth-century drama to a misalliance: an heiress, worth ten thousand pounds, marries a footman. The social distance is not as great as would at first appear, for the girl's father, though he has made a fortune, is of humble origin and has relatives of humble station. Still, his daughter's marriage is a shock to him, though he is reconciled to it by the good sense spoken by her husband (p. 33):

Your Daughter has marry'd a Man of some Learning, and one who has seen a little of the World, and who by his Love to her, and Obedience to you, will try to deserve your Favours. As for my having worn a Livery, let not that grieve you; as I have lived in a great Family, I have seen that no one is respected for what he is, but what he has; the World pays no regard at present to any thing but Money, and if my own Industry shou'd add to your Fortune, so as to entitle any of my Posterity to Grandeur, it will be no reason against making my Son or Grandson a Lord, that his Father or Grandfather, was a Footman.

It is rare indeed for a young man in early-eighteenth-century drama to speak of the possibility of his making a fortune! In the sequel, which is only in part the work of Fielding,[20] the young man asserts, in opposition even to a lord, his personal dignity: at one point he draws his sword against the lord, who attempts to corrupt his foolish wife. This young man is depicted as exemplary—and as remarkably different from the corrupt Londoners of various ranks whom he meets in his efforts to save his wife from the results of her foolish infatuation with town life and to take her back to the country, "where there is still something of old *England* remaining" (pp. 42–43). His father-in-law's pronouncement at the end of the play seems to embody Fielding's dramatic theme (pp. 43–44): "Henceforth, I will know no Degree, no Difference between Men, but what the Standards of Honour and Virtue create: the noblest Birth without these is but a splendid Infamy; and a Footman with these Qualities, is a Man of Honour." Sententious platitudes, perhaps, but they still had something of novelty about them.

Most full-length comedies first produced between 1728 and 1737, by Fielding as well as others, are "genteel" comedies: they include knights, baronets, or lords among their char-

acters, and their love intrigues are conducted with reference
to the terms of the strict marriage settlement that was customary with the nobility and gentry. The social conventions of
fashionable society are generally honored, and the customary
assumption of the rightness of an ordered, hierarchical pattern
of society is usually evident—even though in this era of Fielding, Gay, and others comes the first dramatic suggestion of a
more fundamental social criticism.

But one decisive change there is—the dramatic treatment
of the rich merchant is, in the comedies first produced after
1728, nearly always sympathetic. The dramatists, with few
exceptions, take it for granted that a rich merchant is at home
in fashionable society and that he, or a member of his family,
may marry a member of the landed gentry without presumption. Comedy had not grown democratic, but rather, for the
dramatists, at least, the rich merchant had been assimilated
into the gentry. The Restoration stereotype of the "cit," except in a few instances, had been transformed past recognition.

There were distinctions between merchants, however; or
more properly, such tentative distinctions as had been made
sporadically by earlier dramatists were confirmed. By the
1730's the dramatists, except in some of the trivial farces and
ballad operas, show a clear recognition at least that an overseas
exporter and a tradesman, even though both might be in business, had little in common—that what might be socially pre-
sumptuous for the wife of a shopkeeper was in no way so for
the wife of a man trading to India.

The few examples that comedy from 1728 to 1737 affords
of the traditional duping of a foolish merchant occur in trivial
entertainments: in Philip Bennet's unacted farce, *The Beau's
Adventures* (1733); in Robert Drury's one-act ballad opera,
The Mad Captain (1733), written when the author was seventeen years old;[21] and in Henry Ward's ballad opera, *The
Happy Lovers; Or, The Beau Metamorphosed*, which must be
one of the clumsiest pieces ever produced professionally—if
indeed it was produced, as the title page claims.[22] To be sure,
in Charles Coffey's *The Boarding School; Or, The Sham Captain*, of somewhat higher quality, the familiar merchant dupe
appears in Alderman Nincompoop—but this work is merely
a ballad opera rendering of D'Urfey's *Love for Money; Or,
The Boarding-School* of 1691.[23]

John Hippisley's farce, *A Journey to Bristol* (1731), depends for its effectiveness on a departure from the expected result of a young gentleman's pursuit of a merchant's wife, in this instance the wife having been an acquaintance of the gentleman before her marriage. Hippisley is at pains to establish an expectation that the action will follow the older pattern, portraying the gentleman as a likable rake and the merchant-husband as illiberal and suspicious; but ultimately the wife withstands temptation and, in a manner reminiscent of *The Merry Wives of Windsor*, joins with her husband in discomfiting the gentleman. The farce is in its total satiric intent sympathetic to the merchants, although this is perhaps incidental to its extolling of domestic fidelity and trust.

Most of the comedies of the 1730's, I have said, depict the intrigues of the fashionable—rich merchants, the gentry, and the nobility. At least one comedy appeared, however, which has a City milieu: Matthew Draper's *The Spendthrift* (1731), in which all the major characters belong to the merchant class and live in the City. Allusions to merchant-gentry antagonism occur in dialogue and some gentlemen appear briefly; but class rivalry has no part in the action, which turns rather on a competition between two young men, both of the City, for a City girl. The girl's father, Careful, "An old Citizen, rich and of an affable Temper, easy to be wrought upon, and very indulgent to his Daughter *Jenny*," is portrayed sympathetically, so much so that he bears little resemblance to the stereotype. By his opposition to Young Spend-Thrift, "very wild and extravagant, but of a free, open, generous Spirit," he provides the chief barrier to the resolution of the action, overcome only when Young Spend-Thrift reforms. But Careful has an adequate motive for not wishing the young man to marry his daughter; and he reveals good sense in his discriminating appraisal of social realities—as here in a conversation with his daughter's other suitor, Tawdry, "Alderman Tawdry's son" (I):

CAREFUL: . . . People of the first Rank—
TAWDRY: Beggarly Quality!—(Taking Snuff)
CAREFUL: Have done me the Honour, (as they call it) to court my Daughter.
TAWDRY: They court your Daughter, ha, ha, ha! a good Jest, faith: I wish I cou'd catch 'em at it.
CAREFUL: Not much with my Consent, I must own, for I always

suspect, when they condescend to drive into the dirty City, with their fine Equipages, 'tis to court our Money, more than our Daughters.

Tawdry, it will appear even from this brief exchange, is a merchant-class variant of the type character of the fop. In the denouement, Spend-Thrift's father, "Formerly a rich Citizen of *London*, suppos'd to be drown'd in the *East-Indies*; of a generous Disposition," appears to put his son's affairs in order in preparation for his marriage to Careful's daughter.

James Miller shows in two of his comedies, *The Man of Taste* (1735) and *The Coffee-House* (1737), at once an acknowledgment of the increased prominence of the merchants, an admiration for the personal integrity of many of them, and a residue of resentment at the dislocations in the hierarchical order of society. *The Man of Taste*, based upon Molière's *L'Ecole des maris* and *Les Précieuses ridicules*,[24] is in its social implications the more conservative; it is reminiscent, in fact, of Burnaby's comedies of thirty years before. Miller, a clergyman, customarily includes in his dedicatory epistles self-righteous and somewhat ill-tempered statements charging his contemporaries with social and moral degeneracy; and in the epistle prefixed to *The Man of Taste* he includes insubordination within his range of complaints:

When all Distinctions of Station and Fortune are broke in upon, so that a *Peer* and a *Mechanick* are cloath'd in the same habits, and indulge in the same Diversions and Luxuries: . . . shall not fair and fearless Satire oppose this Outrage upon all Reason and Discretion?

The expectation of conservatism here aroused is fully answered in the comedy, which is, leaving out of account the inconsequential farces and ballad operas previously described, as close to the social assumptions of the Restoration as any comedy of the 1730's.

The two pairs of love intrigues in *The Man of Taste* reflect a distinction between the squirearchy and the merchant class: one pair has to do with the courting of two sisters, the wards respectively of a squire and his brother; and the other with the courting of the daughter and the niece of a rich merchant who has recently moved from the City to the west end. Miller reproves satirically the squire's unenlightened performance as a guardian, contrasting his lack of success with his brother's much greater success; but he portrays both of them as well as their wards genially. His attitude toward the merchant and his family is more complex. Sir Humphry Henpeck, a sympathetically realized variant of the stereotype, is a man of sound good sense, not himself socially affected or ambitious, who has been led by his wife's ambitions to expenditures he regrets (I):

In the first Place [he tells his daughter], I must leave off my Business, which brought me in at least a Thousand a Year, because getting Money was low and servile. Then I must quit my own House, and pay the Duce and all here, because this, it seems, is the Region of Wit and Politeness. And what is worse than all, [I] must throw away, at least, 500 Guineas to get my self knighted, that her Ladyship might be in a Rank above the Vulgar, forsooth. The Family of the *Henpecks* had great Occasion to be thus dignify'd and distinguished, indeed.

Sir Humphry's wife is not flirtatious (perhaps because Miller was unwilling to risk the licentiousness involved in making her so), but she is affected and absurd, and so are her daughter and her niece, who ultimately alienate their suitors. Outraged by his family's follies, Sir Humphry resolves to get himself "unknighted" and to return to his old house in the City—a resolution treated by the dramatist as eminently sensible.

Miller's *Coffee-House* (1737) is socially bolder and dramatically less conventional than *The Man of Taste*, partly because it is an adaptation of a contemporary play, *Le Café*, by Jean-Baptiste Rousseau.[25] It is interesting mainly for its brisk comments on social relations in contemporary London. Hartly, "a Gentleman of the Temple," discusses his plan to marry Kitty with his friend Gaywood, "an Officer" (Sc. 1):

GAYWOOD: . . . But for a Gentleman to marry a Coffee-Man's Daughter—'Sdeath! 'tis a Scandal.

HARTLY: Psha! Interest confounds all Distinctions of that Kind; and if a great many Gentlemen had not marry'd Tradesmen's Daughters, they must have been glad to have turn'd Tradesmen themselves for a Living—provided they had Capacity enough, I mean.

GAYWOOD: That's well provided, truly!

HARTLY: And pray, upon balancing the Account, how am I a sufferer? I am a Gentleman, and poor; she a Coffee-Girl, and rich; why, if I have her Money for my Gentility, troth, I think 'tis a good Bargain.

The consecutive action is given over to working out that bargain—by defeating the plan of Kitty's mother to marry her to Harpie, a rich, old scrivener. Remarkable here is not only the egalitarian note in Hartly's remarks but also the social level of Kitty, the girl he has decided to marry: she is the daughter, not of a wealthy merchant, but of a tradesman, whose wife runs his coffee-house after his death. Kitty, far from having ambition, is delighted with the pleasures of the coffee-house. Her station is lower, I believe, than that of any other sympathetically portrayed heroine in early-eighteenth-century comedy who marries a gentleman; Congreve was eight years dead and the world was changing.

William Popple's *The Lady's Revenge; Or, The Rover Reclaimed* (1734) portrays a merchant respectfully in a plot situation that earlier had customarily evoked contempt. The merchant himself is dead when the play begins, but he is always mentioned respectfully, even by those who had liked him least. His wife, a much younger woman, had married him after having been seduced and betrayed by a gentleman, Sir Harry Lovejoy; and contrary to the expectations and desires of Sir Harry, she had remained true to her husband. The old merchant, lost in a shipwreck, left his widow generously provided for. No longer having the restraint imposed by the marriage vow, she again became the mistress of Sir Harry—until he left her to marry another. The plot, which like that of *The Modern Husband* has novelistic qualities, thus reveals an approximation of a familiar pattern of social rivalry (between merchant and gentleman for the merchant's wife), but the values are new.

In Francis Lynch's *The Independent Patriot; Or, Musical Folly* (1737), a great merchant is completely assimilated into fashionable society. A political satire, the play celebrates manly independence in political affairs, an independence exhibited at once in resistance to the corruptions of the government and to the carping, self-interested criticism of the opposition. The "independent patriot" is Medium, an exemplary character patterned, according to Lynch's dedicatory epistle, after the Earl of Burlington (the character in the play is, however, a commoner, a member of the House of Commons); the great merchant is Alderman Export, presented as a philanthropist and a man of the highest private probity. At the end of the play

Medium marries Export's daughter, with no hint of social incompatibility between the couple.

Elsewhere in the play as well, there are hints of the old stereotypes but the social judgments are new. The villain, Sanguine, a member of Parliament secretly in the employ of Walpole though pretending to rail against him, is a gentleman of extensive holdings in land. Gripeacre, "an old covetous Dissenter" who trades in land, has the superficial qualities of the late-seventeenth-century "cit"; however, he is a caricature not of a businessman but of a corrupt political agent. In Gripeacre the stereotype is reworked in political detail that transforms the social meaning of the character. The intrigues go on amidst talk of corruption, especially political and artistic corruption, reminiscent of Pope's satires written at the same time. The author of the play was not so stern an opponent of Walpole as to be insensitive to contradictions in the arguments of the opposition; but he shared the view of nearly all of the major men of letters that England in the later 1730's was far gone in degeneracy. What is important here, of course, is the point of reference from which the supposed degeneration is measured: no longer the social and political values of the Restoration, but the aspirations of Walpole's England.

The new respectful treatment of the merchant in comedy coincides chronologically with the advent of "sentimentalism." But is there a causal connection between the two phenomena? Let us first define our terms. There is no such genre as "sentimental comedy," in my opinion; "sentimentalism" (in the eighteenth-century sense, which is more specialized than the present sense) is simply an aspect of a great many different kinds of comedy—like racy language, or rustic elements. It must be traced like any other theme: we cannot try to define "sentimental comedy," or look for the first one, or try to determine how many appeared in any given year. Comedy in the early eighteenth century was, as always, sensitive to changes in contemporary patterns of interpretation of behavior, and the period happened to be one when the patterns were changing rapidly—notably, from ethical theories assuming human depravity to those assuming human benevolence. It is the reflection in literature of the new ethical theory that I regard as "sentimentalism" in the eighteenth-century sense. Tragedy and nondramatic literature as well as comedy reflect this theory, as they reflect other contemporary attitudes, including social attitudes, that were undergoing change. The appearance of "sentimentalism" in comedy is only one of several important innovations that came at the end of the seventeenth and in the early eighteenth centuries. To employ the term "sentimental comedy" is misleading, for to do so implies, contrary to the facts, the existence of a large number of comedies having a substantial body of uniform characteristics.[26]

It has been customary to assume that there is a connection between the more respectful treatment of merchants in comedy and the appearance of sentimentalism. The reasoning behind this assumption has two parts: first, that "middle-class" taste came to prevail in the drama; and second, that having come to prevail, it encouraged sentimentalism. There can be no quarrel with the first statement, but the second is difficult to demonstrate, though it may be true. Too often, the demonstration has taken the form of something like social snobbery: that a liking for sentimentalism is evidence of a poorly cultivated taste; that the "middle class" had a less cultivated taste than the gentry and the nobility; and that, since sentimentalism obviously was liked by somebody, it must have been liked by the "middle class." Again, these assumptions may be true. But they merit a close scrutiny.

Some of the most sentimental plays are in their social assumptions the most conspicuously genteel.[27] Is it plausible that the dramatists should have modified the emotional structure of their plays to please new elements in the audience while at the same time emphasizing the decorums of fashionable society—and thus the exclusiveness and the inaccessibility of it? It would seem more likely that the dramatists' concession to those below the rank of the gentry was the more direct one of acknowledging their claim to social consideration. Significantly, I think, there is little correlation between the presence of sentimentalism in the comedies and the more tolerant social views.

Consider the comedies of Colley Cibber. His *Love's Last Shift* (1696), sometimes cited as the first "sentimental comedy," has no characters (except servants) of rank below that of the richer gentry, and its dramatic action is worked out with reference to the property settlements customary with wealthy landowners. The same is true of all his "sentimental" plays—even his last one, *The Provoked Husband* (1728), his completion of Vanbrugh's fragment "A Journey to London." In *The Provoked Husband*, the sentimentalism is in fact concentrated in the action of the characters of highest social station: in Lord Townly's magnanimity toward his wife in her distresses and in her reformation. Cibber actually makes Lord Townly richer than his original in the Vanbrugh fragment and more punctilious in observing the decorums of high life.[28] And in praising Mrs. Oldfield for her performance as Lady Townly, Cibber emphasized her success in portraying the manners of the fashionable:

The qualities she had *acquired* were the *genteel* and the *elegant*. The one in her air and the other in her dress never had her equal on the stage, and the ornaments she herself provided (particularly in this play) seemed in all respects the *paraphonalia* [sic] of a woman of quality.[29]

In plays of other dramatists, too, a concentration on high life—and an insistence, frequently, on its decorums—coincides with sentimentalism. In the younger Cibber's *The Lover* (1730), several sentimental episodes—e.g., a young gentleman's generous response to his sweetheart's feigned loss of her fortune—appear in a play that not only is ostentatiously genteel but contains contemptuous allusions to the merchants. In John Kelly's *The Married Philosopher* (1732), the extreme act of magnanimity of the play, the act that more than any other embodies the dramatist's sentimental interpretation of his subject, is possible only for a character of high station—the voluntary renunciation to another person of an estate of £3,000 a year.

William Popple's *The Double Deceit; Or, A Cure for Jealousy* (1735) is even more to the point. The comedy is mildly sentimental in that the sympathetically portrayed characters are benevolent; and yet the dramatist steadily asserts the propriety of class distinctions. Two young gentlewomen take on the disguise of housemaids to meet appropriately two young gentlemen who come to court them in the disguise of their own servants. The women know the true identity of the men, but the men do not at first know that of the women. The situation gives rise to the following comments on class relationships (IV):

FANNY: Where there is an Inequality, there can be no Freedom; and without Freedom, no agreeable Commerce.

GAYLIFE: But there is a Commerce, my pretty One, which creates a Freedom, let the Difference be ever so great.

HARRIET: 'Tis a Commerce we don't desire to have, and shall never like.

. . .

HARRIET: Sir, to talk to you of Virtue, is to talk to you of a thing, I perceive, you have no Knowledge of, and very little Regard for. I shall therefore wave it, and only tell you, that being born of humble Parents, and having never liv'd better, Servitude, such as ours is, is natural to us, and we have no Inclinations to change.

Since the young women are in fact of gentle birth, the views here expressed have only a theoretical application. However, love or no love, before the young men will marry the young women, they ascertain that they are of appropriate rank. Harriet's reaction to this act of prudence is consonant with the assumptions of the play (V): "I will go so far as to say, if you had taken us on Supposition of being really what we appeared, I should not have lik'd you so well."

Steele, as we know, was at once a sentimentalist and a champion of the merchants. He was a sentimentalist, however, before he took up the cause of the merchants, and if there is a connection between the two aspects of his work—and I believe that there is—it is an indirect one. Steele's first book was a religious tract, *The Christian Hero: An Argument Proving that No Principles but Those of Religion are Sufficient to Make a Great Man* (1701), and he wrote his first play under the influence of Jeremy Collier and other stage reformers. The stage reform movement drew much of the great force it mustered from the mercantile community, with which the reformers were identified by their contemporaries. In an indirect way Steele, in coming under the influence of the reformers, came under that of the merchants; but he did so, it is important to note, only by the route of accepting ethical opinions that many of the merchants held.

Steele's first three comedies, though innocent of the moralistic offenses of which the reformers complained and though in no way disrespectful toward merchants, are socially conservative. Only in *The Conscious Lovers* (1722), produced long after his sentimental bent was established, does Steele openly espouse the merchant cause; and here his social doctrine and his sentimentalism appear independently, even if both contribute to the sober tone of the play. In brief, Steele's social views and his emotional attitudes were separate: they were compatible, but each could exist, and often did, without the other.

The business community, to be sure, encouraged sentimentalism in the negative way of encouraging the dramatic reformers in their protest against the moral attitudes of comedy which were patently anti-benevolistic. At the same time, the merchants were demonstrating the palpable inaccuracy and anachronism of the merchant stereotype, and thus prompting some playwrights to modify their plays. Meanwhile, sentimentalism became prominent in literature in consequence of changes in ethical theories.[80] The history of sentimentalism must be traced in the history of thought, not in the history of society. Social history is relevant to the development of sentimentalism only as it conditioned religious and intellectual history.

Sentimentalism simply cannot be equated with membership in any social class. Members of the upper classes seem to have been quite as much interested in sentimental episodes in literature as their social inferiors. The single most influential propagator of "sentimental" ideas was, after all, the third Earl of Shaftesbury, grandson of the great Earl of Charles II's time. And the most successful literary exploiter of sentimentalism was Henry Fielding—in his novels—the great grandson of an earl and the son of a lieutenant general. Sentimentalism, as derived from the speculations of such thinkers as Shaftesbury, represented an effort at a more accurate psychological interpretation of human action than had been available before, and as such it interested thinking people of all ranks.

The deep social conservatism of early-eighteenth-century comedy was, in the main, undisturbed by the experiments in sentimentalism. Only rarely is there something like a social judgment implicit in the sentimentalism itself.

One such instance is the deemphasis of the property settlement in marriage. Bevil loves and wishes to marry Indiana in *The Conscious Lovers* even though she seemingly is an orphan with no money; and in Theophilus Cibber's *The Lover* (1730) Estace proposes to Inanthe when he thinks she has lost all of her property. The beggar's daughter in Dodsley's *Blind Beggar of Bethnal Green* (1741) wishes fervently to marry her poor sweetheart in preference to a richer admirer; and it is her feeling of obligation to her father that produces the pathos of her situation. In each instance the dramatist regards love as more important than property—though in the denouement of each play the characters are happily rewarded with property as well as love. Sentimentalism, then, may be said to have served in early-eighteenth-century comedy as a mild counterforce to the tradition of strong practicality in financial matters.

Sentimentalism also helped to broaden the social and emotional range of experience customarily treated in comedy. Restoration comedy, after all, treats only a limited part of the experience of a small social group. A strong dramatic tradition and a well-developed critical theory restricted the subjects that appeared in comedy; and if the best of the dramatists, notably Congreve, manage nevertheless to convey an emotional intensity, they do so with respect to a narrow range of human relationships. Their characters are frequently insensitive in situations that would demand an emotional reaction from a normal man; they seem indeed unable to conceive of altruistic emotions not related to sexual love between social equals. For all of its severe liabilities, sentimentalism brought freedom from the emotional inhibitions of the Restoration tradition.

SIX

The Decline of Drama

Comedy takes man in his social relationships as its subject and concentrates on such of those relationships as offer the richest source of affectation. This being so, the paramount theme of Augustan comedy was inevitably the rivalry of merchants and gentry, in one or another of its many variants. The amount of attention lavished on this rivalry was prodigious, and perhaps for this reason the presentation of class relationships came progressively closer, over the years, to historical reality. The stereotypes disappeared, the outrageous distortion came to an end. People could go to the theater and see characters very like themselves.

Yet as comedy gained in the accuracy of its portrayal of society, its quality deteriorated. The deterioration was clear to the Augustans themselves, it has been clear to generations of critics, and it is no less clear today to anyone who reads the comedies of the Augustan canon.

Some of the critics who played variations on the dunciad theme, Dennis and Gildon, for example, associated the decline in drama with the presence in the audience of large numbers of men who had only recently made fortunes. If social conservatism prejudiced the critics' judgment, they must have been right at least to the extent that the newcomers contributed to a heterogeneity of taste that would have been disruptive of dramatic tradition. More important, perhaps, was the change in society of which this change in the audience was a minor consequence. As Fielding among others knew, it was impossible to write comedies like those of Congreve because the life that provided the subject for comedy had changed so radically. Yet if the older aristocratic vein had become an anachronism, there was no reason why other comic veins could not have been exploited. More is involved in the decline of comedy, and of drama generally, than social change—more even than the intermittent eighteenth-century sentimentalism.

For one thing, drama encountered a formidable rival in opera. Italian opera was enormously popular in England after it was introduced in the first decade of the century; it attracted munificent support from the nobility, and even from George I and George II. If some of the complaints about opera were based on dubious aesthetic theory, others were more solidly based on the observed fact that the opera diverted support from the drama.[1] "Between the fashionable *Gout* for Opera's on the one Hand," complains an anonymous critic in *Pasquin*, February 4, 1724, "and the more unaccountable Curiosity for I know not what on the other, all Taste and Relish for the manly and sublime Pleasures of the Stage are as absolutely lost and forgotten, as though such things had never been." An overstatement, but one frequently repeated. The growing prominence of the opera, which not even the burlesque of *The Beggar's Opera* could halt, contributed to the feeling of gloom about the stage that permeates the critical writings of the time.

The theoretical objections made to the opera resemble those of the same years to another rival to the drama—the "entertainments" of singing, dancing, juggling, and especially pantomime that were increasingly offered on the same bill with plays. The vogue of these entertainments can in part be attributed to the "People of sudden Fortunes," to use the phrase of a critic writing in *Mist's Weekly Journal*, October 29, 1726, who blamed them for the popularity of a company of Italian pantomimists. The critics were all but unanimous in agreeing that the distinction between traditional comedy and tragedy, on the one hand, and the supplementary entertainments, on the other, represented the distinction between an appeal to the rational faculties and to the nonrational or merely sensual.[2] But despite the critical opposition, the entertainments flourished and in fact in the decade and a half after 1720 gained in prominence. There was no resisting the trend: "If I am ask'd (after my condemning these Fooleries myself)," wrote Cibber in his *Apology*, "how I came to assent or continue my Share of Expence to them? I have no better Excuse for my Error than confessing it. I did it against my Conscience! and had not Virtue enough to starve by opposing a Multitude that would have been too hard for me."[3] Steele used essentially the same argument in the *Town Talk*, Nos. 1 and 2, as early as 1716. These entertainments did not draw people away from plays, since they appeared on the same program, but they diverted talent and money from the production of new plays and from the revival of old ones not in the current repertories.

Although the number of people who went to the theaters increased somewhat in the early eighteenth century, the number of theaters and hence the number of potential markets for new plays did not increase proportionately. Theatrical monopoly was not, before 1737, strictly enforced; but even so the number of major theaters in operation rarely exceeded four and was more commonly two. Moreover, these theaters were repertory theaters, relying on an established body of old plays for their usual offerings. Theater managers were reluctant to accept new plays, partly, no doubt (as was alleged by disappointed playwrights) because they could fill their houses with old ones without the expense of author's benefit nights. Drury Lane, at the height of its prosperity under the actor-managers, produced from 1714–15 to 1719–20 only from one to four new plays a year; and several of these were produced only after someone in authority had intervened with the managers.[4] The record of Lincoln's Inn Fields and later of Covent Garden is substantially the same.

Moreover, because of the vagaries of the benefit system, a playwright could be assured of no equitable return for his work. Farquhar, dying in poverty after a brilliant and productive career while several of his plays were in the established repertories, is but the most conspicuous of many sufferers from this inept system. It would seem likely that many potentially capable playwrights were prompted by financial considerations alone to choose another field of literary endeavor.

One such field was journalism in its many guises—the newspaper, the political pamphlet, the periodical essay. Journalism gained enormously in strength during this period; and, significantly enough, many of its most distinguished practitioners were part-time playwrights. Steele, credited by his contemporaries with the invention of the periodical essay, began the *Tatler* in 1709 after writing three plays; while writing the *Tatler* he began his last play, which he did not finish until 1722, though in the interim he wrote or was a major contributor to some half dozen series of periodical essays. Addison wrote four acts of *Cato* about the turn of the century, not completing it until 1713 and then only upon the urging of his friends. After its immense success he produced only one other play, *The Drummer* (1716), which, presumably because of its indifferent success, he did not acknowledge in his lifetime. No one can say with authority that journalism diverted Addison from the drama; but it is sufficiently obvious that, possessing some talent for the drama, he expended most of his literary effort in the periodical essay. John Hughes, Lewis Theobald, Ambrose Philips, Aaron Hill, Henry Fielding, Mrs. Manley, and John Gay all were not only playwrights but journalists—many of them presumably at the expense of their work as playwrights. It is at least as possible that some eighteenth-century Shakespeare was buried in Grubstreet as that the cemetery at Stoke Poges harbored a mute, inglorious Milton.

Fielding is a special case, the talented playwright drawn from the drama, not to journalism, but to prose fiction. The result was a gain to English literature, for Fielding's sprightly plays, though they scarcely deserve the oblivion that has overtaken them, are but pale fare alongside *Tom Jones* and *Amelia*. It could be argued that Fielding's novels, and the examples they provided for subsequent novelists, offer more than adequate compensation for the inhibiting effects on the drama of the Licensing Act of 1737.

Indeed, if we want to know why later-eighteenth-century drama came to no more, we may well ponder Fielding's career. Here may be seen in epitome the deflection of creative effort (for political reasons, as was often the case) from the drama to the novel, a deflection that was one of the compelling reasons for the failure of drama in the later eighteenth century. The immense enlargement of the reading public that was both cause and effect of the increased vitality of journalism, and slightly later of the novel, provided the audience and thus the emoluments for able writers that the drama could not provide. The early eighteenth century was the last period in which the drama, acted and printed, was the most popular form of literature. The evolution of domestic tragedy, to choose a striking illustration of the transfer of creative energy from the drama to the novel, from Otway to Southerne to Rowe to Lillo (this genealogy is suggested in the prologue to *George Barnwell*), reaches the point of maturity, not in the work of a dramatist, but in that of a novelist—Richardson.

"The Drama of Sensibility"[5] reaches its climax, not in *The Careless Husband* or *The Conscious Lovers* or *False Delicacy* or even in Edward Moore's *The Gamester*, but in *Clarissa Harlowe*. The significant antecedents of *Clarissa* are to be found, not in earlier prose fiction, but in the drama—in Rowe's *The Fair Penitent* and in Charles Johnson's *Caelia*. Both Rowe and Johnson anticipate the tragic situation of *Clarissa*: that of a virtuous young woman alienated from her family and driven to despair and ultimately to death by the treachery of the man she loves. The parallels of the two plays with *Clarissa* are striking, extending in the case of *Caelia* to such particularity as the enforced confinement of the young woman in a house of ill repute. Yet in neither *The Fair Penitent* nor *Caelia*, for all their preoccupation with the pathos of the heroine's situation, is there an assimilation of the tragic experience sufficiently convincing psychologically to produce high tragedy. The novel, perhaps because it was better adapted to the close analysis of domestic situations or perhaps merely because more able men turned their hand to it, captured decisively the domestic themes and the domestic emotions that had been tentatively explored in the drama, and gave them the artistic fulfillment that was not again to be provided in English drama until our own time.

The novel of the eighteenth century had some advantage over the drama in its very lack of a tradition. Comedy, as I have noted, was conditioned in its plots and characterizations by dramatic tradition, which was reinforced by the generalizing tendency of neoclassical criticism—as represented by the axiom that the dramatist should eschew the particular in favor of the universal. Not possessing a limiting or controlling tradition, the novelist had much more scope for originality. The names of characters in novels are mostly names that emphasize the individuality—the uniqueness—of the characters (e.g., Clarissa Harlowe and Anna Howe).[6] The names of characters in comedy, on the other hand, remain either adjectival ones that isolate generic qualities (e.g., Sir Testy Dolt and Sir Thrifty Gripe) or traditional ones that by long association with certain character types have almost the force of adjectival names (e.g., Belinda and Cynthia). The names are symptomatic.

It is significant that Fielding abandoned the drama for political reasons. By 1737, politics alone had done as much to strangle the theater artistically as all its more direct competitors combined. Scores of plays were written partly or solely for propagandistic reasons, and dramatic criticism, especially in the periodicals, was as often as not preempted by partisan political argument. It was a rare comedy that did not suffer dramatically from its political burden. The most conspicuous exception is *The Beggar's Opera*, in which the political satire provides but one of many strands in a complex critical commentary on society; the play remains a delight even after time has removed the relevance of most of the satire.

In Fielding's political burlesques, on the other hand, the political satire is the living soul; take it away (and two hundred years have done so) and the plays are corpses. This was the usual situation: dramatic material, sometimes very promising dramatic material, was warped or mutilated to suit the ends of propaganda. Dunces and politicians ruled in the theaters, and men of good will were angry. The Licensing Act of 1737 was not Walpole's only sin against the English stage.

Notes

CHAPTER ONE

1. Swift to Pope, letter of January 10, 1721. George Sherburn (ed.), *The Correspondence of Alexander Pope* (Oxford, 1956), II, 70.

2. L. B. Namier, *The Structure of Politics at the Accession of George III* (London, 1929), I, 61n.

3. "Natural and Political Observations and Conclusions upon the State and Condition of England," in *Two Tracts by Gregory King*, ed. George E. Barnett (Baltimore, 1936), p. 31. For a recent discussion of the status of the merchants, see J. H. Plumb, *Sir Robert Walpole: The Making of a Statesman* (London, 1956), pp. 22–29.

4. H. J. Habakkuk, "England," in A. Goodwin (ed.), *The European Nobility in the Eighteenth Century* (London, 1953), pp. 1–2.

5. Daniel Defoe, *A Tour through England and Wales* (Everyman's Library ed.), I, 336. For modern discussion of the investment in stocks, see William Robert Scott, *The Constitution and Finance of English, Scottish and Irish Joint-Stock Companies to 1720* (3 vols., Cambridge, 1910–12); K. G. Davies, "Joint-Stock Investment in the Later Seventeenth Century," *Economic History Review*, IV (1952), 283–301.

6. Habakkuk, in Goodwin (ed.), *European Nobility*, pp. 4–6.

7. Habakkuk "Land Ownership, 1680–1740," *Economic History Review*, X (1940), 11–12.

8. In Barnett (ed.), *Two Tracts*, p. 31. For informed commentary on King and a mid-eighteenth-century statistician, see Peter Mathias, "The Social Structure in the Eighteenth Century: A Calculation by Joseph Massie," *Economic History Review*, X (1957), 30–45.

9. Ralph Davis, "English Foreign Trade, 1660–1700," *Economic History Review*, VII (1954), 161.

10. A. H. John, "War and the English Economy, 1700–1763," *Economic History Review*, VII (1955), 329–44.

11. Norris A. Brisco, *The Economic Policy of Robert Walpole* (New York, 1907), *passim*; John Morley, *Walpole* (London, 1890), p. 168.

12. John Dennis, "To Judas Iscariot, Esq., on the Present State of the Stage," in Edward Niles Hooker (ed.), *The Critical Works of John Dennis* (Baltimore, 1939, 1943), II, 166–67.

13. John Summerson, *Georgian London* (London, 1945), pp. 81ff. For a further account of the growth of London, see Norman G. Brett-James, *The Growth of Stuart London* (London, 1935).

14. Defoe, *Tour through England*, I, 324.

15. Summerson, *Georgian London*, chap. vii.

16. Defoe, *Tour through England*, I, 329.

17. *The Foreigner's Guide: Or a Necessary and Instructive Companion Both for the Foreigner and Native, in Their Tour through the Cities of London and Westminster* (London, 1729), p. 8.

18. M. Dorothy George, *London Life in the Eighteenth Century* (London, 1925), pp. 2–3.

19. Defoe, *Tour through England*, I, 336.

20. Epilogue Spoken at the Opening of the New House, March 26, 1674. In William Bradford Gardner, *The Prologues and Epilogues of John Dryden* (New York, 1951), pp. 62–63.

21. Colley Cibber, *An Apology for the Life of Mr. Colley Cibber*, ed. Robert W. Lowe (London, 1889), I, 314.

22. *Ibid.*, II, 172.

23. *Ibid.*, I, 322.

24. George, *London Life*, pp. 287–89, 395–96.

25. Henri de Valbourg Misson, *Mémoires et observations faites par un voyageur en Angleterre* (la Haye, 1698), pp. 63–64.

26. George Farquhar, *A Discourse upon Comedy . . .* , ed. Louis A. Strauss (Boston, 1914), p. 6.

27. *Apology for Cibber*, I, 234, 234n.

28. John Dennis, *A Large Account of the Taste in Poetry*, in *Critical Works*, I, 293.

29. *The Life of Mr. Thomas Betterton* (London, 1710), p. 13.

30. Act IV.

31. Act III.

32. Harry William Pedicord, *The Theatrical Public in the Time of Garrick* (New York, 1954), chap. ii.

CHAPTER TWO

1. As ably demonstrated by L. C. Knights in *Drama and Society in the Age of Jonson* (New York, n.d.), *passim*.

2. R. H. Tawney, *Religion and the Rise of Capitalism* (London, 1926), p. 231.

3. *Ibid.*, p. 150.

4. *Ibid.*, p. 144.

5. Cf. Joseph Spence, *Anecdotes, Observations, and Characters, of Books and Men*, ed. Samuel Weller Singer, 2d ed. (London, 1858), p. 121.

6. Arthur Storrey Trace, Jr., "The Continuity of Opposition to the Theater in England from Gosson to Collier" (unpublished dissertation, Stanford University, 1954), p. 11.

7. Joseph Wood Krutch, *Comedy and Conscience after the Restoration*, 2d ed. (New York, 1949), pp. 92–94.

8. Quoted from Richard C. Boys, *Sir Richard Blackmore and the Wits: A Study of "Commendatory Verses on the Author of the Two Arthurs and the Satyr against Wit"* (*1700*) (Ann Arbor, Mich., 1949), p. 15.

9. T. S. Ashton, *An Economic History of England: The Eighteenth Century* (London, 1955), pp. 19–20.

10. Prologue to William Taverner, *The Female Advocates; Or, The Frantic Stock-Jobber* (London, 1713).

11. See Edward Niles Hooker, "Pope on Wit: *The Essay on Criticism*," in Richard Foster Jones *et al.*, *The Seventeenth Century* (Stanford, 1951), pp. 225–46. On the intellectual background of "wit," see Thomas H. Fujimura, *The Restoration Comedy of Wit* (Princeton, N.J., 1952), chaps. ii and iii.

12. See Boys, *Sir Richard Blackmore*, p. 15; Robert M. Krapp, "Class Analysis of a Literary Controversy," *Science and Society*, X (1946), 80–92; Albert Rosenberg, *Sir Richard Blackmore* (Lincoln, Neb., 1953), pp. 39–70.

13. Reprinted by Augustan Reprint Society (Los Angeles, 1946), p. 214.

14. *Ibid.*, p. 191.

15. In J. E. Spingarn (ed.), *Critical Essays of the Seventeenth Century* (Oxford, 1909), III, 229.

16. *Ibid.*, p. 234.

17. *Ibid.*, p. 230.

18. *Ibid.*, p. 231

19. Boys, *Sir Richard Blackmore*, p. 5.

20. Quoted from *ibid.*, p. 7.

21. See *ibid.*, *passim*.

22. Quoted from *ibid.*, p. 16.

23. *Epistle*, p. 1.

24. Quoted from William Lee, *Daniel Defoe: His Life, and Recently Discovered Writings* (London, 1869), I, 40.

25. "The Present State of Wit," Augustan Reprint Society (Los Angeles, 1947), p. 3.

26. *The Fears of the Pretender Turn'd into the Fears of Debauchery with a Hint to Richard Steele, Esq.*

27. No. 339.

28. Rae Blanchard (ed.), *Tracts and Pamphlets by Richard Steele* (Baltimore, 1944), pp. 311–12.

29. In Spingarn (ed.), *Critical Essays*, III, 231.

30. In *ibid.*, p. 256.

31. See Aubrey L. Williams, *Pope's Dunciad: A Study of Its Meaning* (Baton Rouge, La., 1955), p. 15; and also Hugo M. Reichard, "Pope's Social Satire: Belles-Lettres and Business," *PMLA*, LXVII (1952), 420–34.

32. See George Sherburn, "*The Dunciad*, Book IV," *Studies in English, Department of English, the University of Texas*, 1944 (Austin, 1945), pp. 174–90.

33. See Dennis, *Critical Works*, I, 491.

34. *Ibid.*, p. 290.

35. *Ibid.*, p. 291.

36. See above, pp. 16–17.

37. *Critical Works*, I, 293–94.

38. John Robert Moore tentatively ascribes this work to Charles Gildon; see "Gildon's Attack on Steele and Defoe in *The Battle of the Authors*," *PMLA*, LXVI (1951), 534–38.

39. Dedicatory Epistle (an ironical one to Count Heidegger).

40. See Dane Farnsworth Smith, *Plays about the Theatre in England from "The Rehearsal" in 1671 to the Licensing Act in 1737* (New York and London, 1936), *passim*.

41. See Richard Hindry Barker, *Mr. Cibber of Drury Lane* (New York, 1939), pp. 158–59; Allardyce Nicoll, *A History of Early Eighteenth Century Drama*, 3d ed. (Cambridge, England, 1952), p. 316.

42. Sherburn, *Studies in English*, pp. 174–90.

43. Smith, *Plays about the Theater*, pp. 140–50.

CHAPTER THREE

1. "One peculiarity of the stage at this time was that nearly all the dramatists were Whigs . . . Congreve, Addison, Rowe, Mrs. Centlivre and Colley Cibber were Whigs, and Farquhar, Vanbrugh and Steele were not only Whigs but soldiers. But the politics of the audience was by no means entirely Whig." G. M. Trevelyan, *England under Queen Anne* (London, 1930–34), I, 86.

2. See Robert Walcott, *English Politics in the Early Eighteenth Century* (Oxford, 1956), *passim*.

3. H. J. Habakkuk, "Marriage Settlements in the Eighteenth Century," in *Transactions of the Royal Historical Society*, XXXII (1950), 24.

4. In the dialogue of Charles Johnson's *The Village Opera* (I), there is an informative statement of contemporary customs of reciprocity in jointures and dowries.

5. In Barnett (ed.), *Two Tracts*, p. 31.

6. For discussion of the social and literary background of Congreve's comedies, see Kathleen M. Lynch, *The Social Mode of Restoration Comedy* (New York, 1926), especially chap. vii.

7. In his dedicatory epistle prefixed to *The Way of the World*, Congreve discusses his distinction between a "Witwoud" and a "Truewit."

8. See above, p. 27.

9. Nicoll, *Early Eighteenth Century Drama*, p. 171.

10. The play was reprinted by the Augustan Reprint Society (Los Angeles, 1952), with an introduction by Vinton A. Dearing.

11. For a discussion of Baker's career as a dramatist, see John Harrington Smith's Introduction to Baker's *The Fine Lady's Airs* (A.R.S., Los Angeles, 1950); for one of Burnaby's, see F. E. Budd's Introduction to his edition of *The Dramatic Works of William Burnaby* (London, 1931).

12. In Wycherley's *The Gentleman Dancing Master*, however, which was produced as early as 1671 or 1672, there is an allusion to merchants leaving the City (I). Hippolita is speaking to Mrs. Caution: "Come, come, do not blaspheme this masquerading Age, like an ill-bred City-Dame, whose Husband is half broke by living in *Covent-Garden*, or who has been turn'd out of the *Temple* or *Lincoln's-Inn* upon a masquerading Night."

13. Cf. Driver's debate with his wife's gentle-born cousin on the respective claims of money and birth (II).

14. The satire here probably includes a glance at mercantilist economic theory. Nicknack violates an important precept of contemporary nationalistic economic doctrine by importing flagrantly nonessential luxuries. See Jacob Viner, *Studies in the Theory of International Trade* (New York, 1937), p. 30.

15. Richard Hindry Barker, *Mr. Cibber of Drury Lane* (New York, 1939), pp. 39, 68. *The Double Gallant* also includes borrowings from Mrs. Centlivre's *Love at a Venture*.

16. In a conversation between Lord Morelove and Lady Easy in the fifth act.

17. See above, pp. 31–33.

18. Steele took suggestions for the character from Molière's *Les Précieuses ridicules*.

19. For an account of her career, see John Wilson Bowyer, *The Celebrated Mrs. Centlivre* (Durham, N.C., 1952).

20. Defoe, *Tour through England*, I, 336.

21. See L. B. Namier, *England in the Age of the American Revolution* (London, 1930), pp. 17–18.

22. See Habakkuk in Goodwin (ed.), *European Nobility*, p. 4.

23. See below, pp. 116–17.

24. See John Harrington Smith, "Tony Lumpkin and the Country Booby Type in Antecedent English Comedy," *PMLA*, LVIII (1943), 1038–49.

25. *Ibid.*

26. Baker's comedies with locales at Oxford and Hampstead Heath (*An Act at Oxford* and *Hampstead-Heath*), however, are merely variants of what is substantially the same play. See Smith's Introduction cited in note 11 above.

CHAPTER FOUR

1. W. R. Ward, *The English Land Tax in the Eighteenth Century* (London, 1953), pp. 17–29; Habakkuk, "English Landownership," *Economic History Review*, X, 2–17.

2. See Émile Legouis, "Les deux Sir Roger de Coverley: celui de Steele et celui d'Addison," *Revue germanique*, II (1906), 453–71.

3. George Macaulay Trevelyan, *England under Queen Anne*, III, 108; see also Keith Feiling, *A History of the Tory Party, 1640–1714* (Oxford, 1924), p. 432.

4. No. 44 (June 7, 1711).

5. Peter Smithers, *The Life of Joseph Addison* (Oxford, 1954), p. 248.

6. Jehan Maintrieu, *Le Traité d'Utrecht et les polémiques du commerce anglais* (Paris, 1909); Viner, *Studies in International Trade*, pp. 115–18.

7. See John Loftis, *Steele at Drury Lane* (Berkeley and Los Angeles, 1952), pp. 183–93.

8. See *ibid.*, pp. 195–213.

9. British Museum, Additional MS 5145 C, fol. 198. Printed by John Nichols in *The Epistolary Correspondence of Richard Steele* (London, 1809), p. 648n.

10. Nicoll, *Early Eighteenth Century Drama*, p. 299.

11. See above, pp. 64–68.

12. Cf. Steele, *Englishman* (1st series), No. 4 (October 13, 1713).

13. Cibber's immediate source may have been Thomas Wright's *Female Virtuosos* (1693), which is itself an adaptation of *Les Femmes savantes*. See Barker, *Cibber*, pp. 126–27; and William Henry Irving, *John Gay, Favorite of the Wits* (Durham, N.C., 1940), pp. 188–90.

14. For further discussion of the expression of Whig political views in eighteenth-century literature, see Cecil A. Moore, "Whig Panegyric Verse: A Phase of Sentimentalism" (first published in *PMLA*, XLI [1926]), in *Backgrounds of English Literature, 1700–1760* (Minneap-

olis, 1953), pp. 104–44; Clement Ramsland, "Whig Propaganda in the Theater, 1700–1742" (unpublished dissertation, University of Minnesota, 1940); Samuel Kliger, *The Goths in England: A Study in Seventeenth and Eighteenth Century Thought* (Cambridge, Mass., 1952), especially Introduction.

15. For an excellent discussion of farce in the eighteenth century, see Leo Hughes, *A Century of English Farce* (Princeton, N.J., 1956).

16. Nicoll, *Early Eighteenth Century Drama*, p. 210.

17. *Ibid.*, p. 214; the preface to the play.

18. John Loftis, "The London Theaters in Early-Eighteenth-Century Politics," *Huntington Library Quarterly*, XVIII (1955), 365–93.

19. Anonymous, *Exchange-Alley; Or, The Stock-Jobber Turned Gentleman, with the Humours of our Modern Projectors* (London, 1720), p. 34.

20. Cf. Habakkuk, "English Landownership." *Economic History Review*, X, 11–12.

21. Rae Blanchard (ed.), *Correspondence of Richard Steele* (Oxford, 1941), pp. 505–18.

22. Nicoll, *Early Eighteenth Century Drama*, pp. 139–40.

23. Loftis, "The London Theaters in Early-Eighteenth-Century Politics," pp. 385–86.

24. Bowyer, *Centlivre*, pp. 160–62.

25. Cf. Lucy Stuart Sutherland, *A London Merchant, 1695–1774* (Oxford, 1933), pp. 5–6.

CHAPTER FIVE

1. For an account of politics in the 1720's, see Charles Bechdolt Realey, *The Early Opposition to Sir Robert Walpole, 1720–1727* (Philadelphia, 1931), and Keith Feiling, *The Second Tory Party, 1714–1832* (London, 1938), pp. 13–38.

2. See David Harrison Stevens, "Some Immediate Effects of *The Beggar's Opera*," *Manly Anniversary Studies in Language and Literature* (Chicago, 1923), pp. 180–89.

3. See below, pp. 127–32.

4. See Nicoll, *Early Eighteenth Century Drama*, pp. 271–73.

5. Edmund McAdoo Gagey, *Ballad Opera* (New York, 1937), pp. 81–83.

6. As noted above (p. 98), the character Freehold in Charles Johnson's *The Country Lasses* (1715) cites the Latin satirists on Rome in his railing review of London life.

7. William Robert Irwin, *The Making of Jonathan Wild* (New

York, 1941) contains a valuable account of the literature of the London underworld.

8. Cf. Bertrand H. Bronson, *"The Beggar's Opera,"* in *Studies in the Comic* (University of California Publications in English, 1941), pp. 227–29.

9. Cf. an open letter printed in the *Daily Gazeteer*, May 7, 1737. In his life of Gay, Samuel Johnson discusses the contemporary charges that *The Beggar's Opera* had a pernicious influence.

10. See Gagey, *Ballad Opera*. Note especially Gagey's "Bibliography of Ballad Operas," pp. 237–44.

11. The play, however, seems to have been based immediately, and perhaps exclusively, on an English ballad. See Ralph Straus, *Robert Dodsley: Poet, Publisher, and Playwright* (London, 1910), pp. 57–58.

12. Nicoll, *Early Eighteenth Century Drama,* p. 146.

13. Julio is, of course, a character in the literary tradition of primitivism: see Lois Whitney, *Primitivism and the Idea of Progress in English Popular Literature of the Eighteenth Century* (Baltimore, 1934), pp. 75–78.

14. Nicoll, *Early Eighteenth Century Drama,* pp. 145–46.

15. *The Levee. A Farce . . . As it was Offer'd to, and accepted for Representation by the Master of the Old-House in Drury-Lane, but by the Inspector of Farces denied a License* (London, 1741).

16. Hughes includes a salutary warning against confounding Fielding's burlesques and his farces: *A Century of English Farce,* pp. 259–60.

17. See Habakkuk in *Economic History Review*, X, 2–17.

18. See F. W. Bateson, *English Comic Drama, 1700–1750* (Oxford, 1929), pp. 115–16.

19. For a discussion of Fielding's social philosophy, see Archibald Bolling Shepperson, "Fielding on Liberty and Democracy," *English Studies in Honor of James Southall Wilson* (Charlottesville, Va., 1951), pp. 265–75; and George Sherburn, "Fielding's Social Outlook," *Philological Quarterly*, XXXV (1956), 1–23.

20. Wilbur L. Cross, *The History of Henry Fielding* (New Haven, 1918), I, 368.

21. Gagey, *Ballad Opera,* p. 116.

22. Cf. *ibid.,* p. 124.

23. *Ibid.,* p. 114.

24. Nicoll, *Early Eighteenth Century Drama,* p. 144.

25. *Ibid.,* p. 146.

26. I differ fundamentally with the conception of sentimental drama as a "genre" expressed by Arthur Sherbo in his *English Sentimental Drama*

(East Lansing, Michigan, 1957). For a fuller statement of my views on the subject, see my recent review of his book in *Modern Language Notes,* LXXIV (1959), 447–50.

27. Mr. Sherbo anticipates some of my conclusions on this subject. Cf. *Sentimental Drama,* pp. 13–14.

28. Cf. Barker, *Cibber,* pp. 143–44.

29. Quoted from *ibid.,* p. 148.

30. For discussion of the religious and intellectual background of sentimentalism, see Ronald S. Crane, "Suggestions toward a Genealogy of 'The Man of Feeling,'" *ELH, A Journal of English Literary History,* I (1934), 205–30; Ernest L. Tuveson, "The Importance of Shaftesbury," *ELH, A Journal of English Literary History,* XX (1953), 267–99.

CHAPTER SIX

1. For a discussion of the grounds for the criticism of opera, see Siegmund A. E. Betz, "The Operatic Criticism of the *Tatler* and *Spectator,*" *Musical Quarterly,* XXXI (1945), 318–30.

2. See Emmett L. Avery, "The Defense and Criticism of Pantomimic Entertainment in the Early Eighteenth Century," *ELH, A Journal of English Literary History,* V (1938), 127–45.

3. II, 181–82.

4. Loftis, *Steele at Drury Lane,* pp. 84–85.

5. Ernest Bernbaum's phrase: *The Drama of Sensibility* (Boston, 1915).

6. This point is made by Ian Watt in *The Rise of the Novel* (London, 1957), pp. 18–21.

Index

Addison, Joseph, 32, 78, 81, 83; and critical controversy, 31, 33, 37; attitude toward merchants, 34, 79–81 *passim*; quoted, 34, 79–80
—— *Cato*, 136; *The Drummer*, 81, 96–97, 136; *The Freeholder*, 70
Ancients and moderns, controversy over, 37, 38
Anne, Queen of England, 2, 4, 11, 77, 83, 86, 88
Arbuthnot, John, 83
Audiences: changes in, 9, 15–19, 37; effect on drama, 43, 54–68 *passim*, 133

Baker, Thomas, 3, 26, 61, 66, 75; treatment of social relationships, 44, 57–61
—— *An Act at Oxford*, 27, 144n.26; *The Fine Lady's Airs*, 60–61; *Hampstead Heath*, 59–60, 144n.26; *The Humour of the Age*, 17, 57, 58; *Tunbridge Walks*, 57
Battle of the Authors, The, 37–38, 39
Baxter, Richard, 22
Beaumont, Francis, and John Fletcher: their *The Knight of the Burning Pestle*, 22
Bennet, Philip: *The Beau's Adventures*, 122
Betterton, Thomas, 14
Blackmore, Sir Richard, 25, 32; and the controversy over wit, 28–32; attitude toward merchants, 34
—— *Creation*, 32; *Essay upon Wit*, 28–29; *King Arthur*, 29–30; *Prince Arthur*, 30; Preface, 29, 34; *Satire against Wit*, 30, 32
Blanch, John: his *The Beaux Merchant*, 85–86
Bolingbroke, Henry St. John, Viscount, 44, 78, 80, 81
Booth, Barton, 102
Breval, Captain John: his *The Play is the Plot*, 99, 100
British Journal, or the Traveller, The, 33
British Merchant, The, 81
British Stock-Jobbers, The, 96

Brown, Tom, 26; editor of *Commendatory Verses*, 30
Buckingham, George Villiers, second duke of: his *The Rehearsal*, 39
Bullock, Christopher: his *Cobbler of Preston*, 98; *Woman's Revenge*, 106
Bunyan, John, 22
Burnaby, William, 3, 57, 61, 75, 124; treatment of social relationships, 44, 57–59
—— *Ladies' Visiting Day*, 26–27, 58–59, 61, 62; *Love Betrayed*, 57; *The Modish Husband*, 58; *The Reformed Wife*, 17–18, 58, 61

Carey, Henry: his *Chrononhotonthologos*, 38
Centlivre, Susannah, 3, 57, 61, 75, 88, 90; treatment of social relationships, 44, 64–68, 86–88
—— *The Basset-Table*, 66; *A Bold Stroke for a Wife*, 87, 93, 95; *The Busy Body*, 64, 66–67, 87; *The Gamester*, 66; *The Gotham Election*, 99; *Love at a Venture*, 143n.15; *Love's Contrivance*, 65–66; *The Man's Bewitched*, 76; *Marplot*, 66–67; *The Platonic Lady*, 18, 66; *The Wonder, a Woman Keeps a Secret*, 87–88, 93
Cervantes, 120
Character types: booby squire, 43, 44, 50, 69–76 *passim*, 100; fop, 57, 97, 124; merchant. *See* Merchant class, "Cit"
Charles I, King of England, 25
Charles II, King of England, 16, 25, 36, 131
Chetwood, William Rufus: his *The Stock-Jobbers; Or, The Humours of Exchange-Alley*, 96
Cibber, Colley, 26, 38, 57, 65, 75, 90, 102; quoted, 14–15, 129; and Pope's *Dunciad*, 36, 39, 40; and dramatic reform, 37, 33, 63; treatment of social relationships, 38, 61–62; burlesqued by Fielding, 39–40; his later plays, 80–90; and sentimentalism, 128–29
—— *Apology*, 134; *The Careless Husband*, 63, 137; *Damon and Phillida*,

103; *The Double Gallant*, 61–62, 143n.15; *Love in a Riddle*, 103; *Love Makes a Man*, 63; *Love's Last Shift*, 48, 70, 128–29; *The Provoked Husband*, 129; *The Refusal*, 88–90, 93, 95

Cibber, Theophilus, 39–40; his *The Lover*, 129, 132; *Patie and Peggie*, 104

"Cit": change in meaning of term, 18, 122, 127

Coffey, Charles: his *The Beggar's Wedding*, 106; *The Boarding School*, 122; *Southwark Fair*, 105

Collier, Jeremy, 3, 130; and reform of the stage, 24–34 *passim*, 65; attitude toward merchant class, 34, 41; his *A Short View of the Immorality . . . of the English Stage*, 24–34 *passim*

Comedian, or Philosophical Enquirer, The, 15

Commendatory Verses, on the Author of the Two Arthurs, 30, 32

Congreve, William, 2, 20, 26, 60, 61, 68, 84, 114, 117, 126, 132, 133; treatment of social relationships, 23–24, 35, 43, 44–54 *passim*; as a Whig, 44; treatment of rural characters, 69–70

—— *The Double Dealer*, 45, 47, 52, 69; *Love for Love*, 46, 52, 69–70; *The Old Bachelor*, 23–24, 50, 52, 69; *The Way of the World*, 46, 52, 53, 69, 70, 143n.7; dedication, 49–50

Cooke, Thomas: his "The Battle of the Poets," 39

Country settings: increase in use of, 96–100; and the rural-urban conflict, 103–8 *passim*; and Fielding's plays, 120–21

Covent Garden Theater, 13, 14, 30, 102, 103, 135

Crauford, David: his *Courtship à la Mode*, 56

Criticism, dramatic: and reform of the stage, 24–42 *passim*, 63, 65; in early 18th century plays, 38–41; and the merchant class, 81; and Steele's *The Conscious Lovers*, 83–84

Cromwell, Oliver, 22, 23

Dancourt, Florent Carton: his *Les Bourgeoises à la Mode*, 50

Davenant, Sir William: his *Love and Honour*, 92

Davys, Mary: her *The Northern Heiress*, 99

Defoe, Daniel, 32, 96; quoted, 5, 11, 13; ties with the merchant class, 34, 37, 38; and *The Mercator*, 81

—— *The Pacificator*, 31; *The Review*, 26; *Robinson Crusoe*, 38

Dekker, Thomas: his *The Shoemaker's Holiday*, 22, 112

De L'Isle, L.F., 114

Dennis, John, 12, 15, 26, 33, 39, 82, 133; quoted, 10, 16–17; as an aesthetic critic, 36–37

—— *The Causes of the Decay and Defects of Dramatic Poetry*, 36; *A Large Account of the Taste in Poetry*, 36–37; *The Usefulness of the Stage*, 33

Deposing and Death of Queen Gin, The (anon. comedy), 106

Dilke, Thomas: his *The City Lady*, 54–55; *The Lover's Luck*, 55; *The Pretenders*, 56

Discommendatory Verses, 30

Dodsley, Robert, 102, 109, 113; treatment of social relationships, 110–13

—— *The Blind Beggar of Bethnal Green*, 104, 112, 132; *The King and the Miller of Mansfield*, 104, 110–12; *Sir John Cockle at Court*, 104, 112; *The Toy Shop*, 112

Doggett, Thomas: his *The Country Wake*, 75

Dorman, John: his *Sir Roger de Coverley; Or, The Merry Christmas*, 105

Dorset Garden Theater, 13, 14

Draper, Matthew: his *The Spendthrift*, 123–24

Drury, Robert: his *The Mad Captain*, 122

Drury Lane Theater, 10, 13, 14, 37, 38, 61, 93–94, 99, 102–3, 135

Dryden, John, 30–31, 82; quoted, 14; his *The Fables*, 25; *MacFlecknoe*, 36

Duck, Stephen, 39

Duke's Theater, The, 13

D'Urfey, Thomas: his *Love for Money*, 122; *The Richmond Heiress*, 55

Englishman, The, 83, 94–95

Etherege, Sir George, 117

Examiner, The. *See* Swift, Jonathan

Exchange-Alley; Or, The Stock-Jobber Turned Gentleman (anon. farce), 96, 145n.19

Farquhar, George, 61, 68, 69, 82, 84, 135; treatment of class relationships, 35, 42–54 *passim*; treatment of rural characters, 44, 72–74
——— *The Beaux' Stratagem,* 46–49 *passim,* 72–75 *passim,* 90, 96; *The Constant Couple,* 27, 46–47 *passim,* 51–52, 54, 72; *A Discourse upon Comedy,* 16; *Love and a Bottle,* 47, 72; *The Recruiting Officer,* 46–49 *passim,* 54, 72–75 *passim,* 96; *Sir Harry Wildair,* 54; *The Twin Rivals,* 43, 45–49 *passim*

Fielding, Henry, 36, 40, 70, 101, 102, 106, 109, 122, 131, 133, 136, 138; treatment of social relationships, 114–21; compared with Congreve, 117–18
——— Plays: *The Author's Farce,* 18, 38–41 *passim,* 115, 116; *The Covent-Garden Tragedy,* 106, 116, 117; *Don Quixote in England,* 99, 115, 120; *The Intriguing Chambermaid,* 116; *The Letter Writers,* 116; *The Lottery,* 117; *Love in Several Masques,* 115–19 *passim; Miss Lucy in Town,* 117, 120, 121; *The Modern Husband,* 98, 116–17 *passim,* 119–20, 126; *An Old Man Taught Wisdom,* 120–21; *Pasquin,* 38–42, 99, 115, 116; *Rape upon Rape,* 117; *The Temple Beau,* 115, 116–19 *passim; Tom Thumb,* 38, 39; *The Universal Gallant,* 116–17 *passim,* 120; *The Wedding Day,* 116
——— Novels: *Amelia,* 116, 119, 136; *Jonathan Wild,* 115–16; *Joseph Andrews,* 116, 120; *Tom Jones,* 70, 98, 116, 136
——— Other works: *The Champion,* 115; *The Journal of a Voyage to Lisbon,* 115

Fleetwood, Charles, 102

Fletcher, John: his *The Custom of the Country,* 98

Freeholder's Journal, The, 97

Garrick, David, 15, 19

Gay, John, 31, 98, 101, 102, 114, 122, 136
——— *The Beggar's Opera,* 3, 38, 72, 90, 101–10 *passim,* 134, 138, 146n.9; *Polly,* 106–8; *Three Hours After Marriage,* 38; *The What D'Ye Call It,* 38

Gentry: in 18th century life, 4, 5, 77–82; treatment of in comedy, 38, 68–76 *passim,* 84–85, 86, 88–90, 122–27

George I, King of England, 12, 93, 98–102 *passim,* 134

George II, King of England, 101, 134

Gildon, Charles, 17, 82, 133

Godolphin, Sidney, Earl, 78

Goldsmith, Oliver, 75, 109

Goodman's Fields Theater, 15, 33, 102

Gosson, Stephen, 24

Griffin, Benjamin: his *Love in a Sack,* 90–91

Guardian, The, 32, 83

Hamilton, Newburgh: his *The Petticoat-Plotter,* 90

Harley, Robert, Earl of Oxford, 44, 78

Harris, Joseph: his *The City Bride,* 56–57

Hawker, Essex: his *The Wedding,* 105

Hawlings, Francis: his *It Should Have Come Sooner,* 95

Haymarket Theater, 39, 102

Higden, Henry: his *The Wary Widow,* 56

Highmore, John, 102

Hill, Aaron, 136

Hippisley, John: his *A Journey to Bristol,* 123; *Flora,* 105; *A Sequel to the Opera of Flora,* 105

Hogarth, William, 103, 106, 114

Hughes, John, 136

Intriguing Widow, The, 74

James II, King of England, 25

Johnson, Charles, 44, 99
——— *Caelia,* 98, 137; *The Cobbler of Preston,* 98; *The Country Lasses,* 81, 95, 96, 98, 145 n.6; *Love in a Forest,* 98; *The Village Opera,* 98, 142 n.4

Johnson, Samuel, 146 n.9

Jonson, Ben, 20, 21, 51, 55

Journalism: and the decline of drama, 135–36

Kelly, Hugh: his *False Delicacy*, 137
Kelly, John: his *The Married Philosopher*, 129; *Timon in Love*, 113–14
King, Gregory, 4, 6, 47
Kit-Cat Club, 83

Landed Property Qualification Bill of 1711, 34, 80
Law, William, 32
Licensing Act of 1737, 101, 136, 138
Lillo, George, 1, 2, 105, 116, 136; his *The London Merchant; Or...George Barnwell*, 33, 104, 136; *Silvia*, 104–5
Lincoln's Inn Fields Theater, 13, 14, 93–94, 98, 102–3 *passim*, 135
Little Theater in the Haymarket, 102
Locke, John, 29
London: it growth, 9–15, 20, 21; and Pope's *Dunciad*, 36; and rural-urban relations in the drama, 68–76 *passim*, 103–8 *passim*; and Fielding's plays, 114, 116–20
Lottery, The (anon. comedy), 106
Lynch, Francis: his *The Independent Patriot*, 126–27

Manley, Mary de la Rivière, 136
Marlborough, John Churchill, Duke of, 78
Massinger, Philip, 20, 21, 51, 55; his *The City Madam*, 20; *A New Way to Pay Old Debts*, 22
Mercator, The, 81
Merchant class: in 18th century life, 1–9, 21, 33, 77–82; literary treatment of, 1–2, 3, 20–24, 33–35, 38, 44, 54–68, 81–82, 85–86, 90–95, 102, 122–27; and literary criticism, 26–27, 29, 38, 41, 81, 82; and Pope, 35–36; and Vanbrugh, 49, 51; and Farquhar, 49, 51–52; and Congreve, 49, 52–53; and Cibber, 61–62, 88–90; and Steele, 63–64, 84–85; and Centlivre, 64–68, 86–88; and Fielding, 115–16; and sentimentalism, 128–32
Middleton, Thomas, 21; his *A Mad World, My Masters*, 98
Miller, James, 102, 124–26; his *Art and Nature*, 113; *The Coffee-House*, 124, 125–26; *The Man of Taste*, 102, 124, 125
Mist's Weekly Journal, 134
Modern Poetasters, The (anon. satire), 96

Molière: his *L'Ecole des maris*, 124; *Les Femmes savantes*, 56, 88, 144 n.13; *Le Médecin malgré lui*, 65; *Les Précieuses ridicules*, 124, 143 n.18
Molloy, Charles: his *The Coquet*, 92, 95; *The Half-Pay Officer*, 92; *The Perplexed Couple*, 92
Montesquieu, Charles de, 109
Moore, Edward: his *The Gamester*, 137
Moore-Smythe, James: his *The Rival Modes*, 92–93
Motteux, Peter Anthony: his *Love's a Jest*, 75, 76

Neoclassicism, 37, 38, 82, 84, 137
Novel, the: and the decline of drama, 136–37

Odell, Thomas: his *The Chimera*, 95–96
Odingsell, Gabriel: his *The Capricious Lovers*, 99
Opera, Italian: and the decline of drama, 134
Otway, Thomas, 136
Oxford, Robert Harley, Earl of, 44, 78

Pasquin (periodical), 134
Pastoral convention: reflected in drama of 1728–37, 103–8 *passim*
Philips, Ambrose, 136
Phillips, Edward: his *The Livery Rake and Country Lass*, 105
Pix, Mary: her *The Beau Defeated*, 56, 74
"Pleasures of the Town, The." See Fielding, Henry, *The Author's Farce*
Pope, Alexander, 82, 114, 127; as a critic, 1–2, 24, 35, 38, 39
———*The Dunciad*, 24, 35–41 *passim*; *Epistles to Several Persons*, 1–2, 101; *Essay on Criticism*, 31; *Imitations of Horace*, 1, 101; *Peri Bathous*, 36; *The Rape of the Lock*, 1, 3
Popple, William: his *The Double Deceit*, 129–30; *The Lady's Revenge*, 126
Powell, George: his *The Cornish Comedy*, 56, 74, 75; *A Very Good Wife*, 55
Prynne, William, 31, 24–25; his *Histriomastix*, 25
Pulteney, William, 101

Ramsay, Allan: his *The Gentle Shepherd*, 103–4

Ravenscroft, Edward: his *The Canterbury Guests*, 56, 74, 75
Review, The, 26
Rich, John, 14, 102, 103
Richardson, Samuel, 137; his *Clarissa*, 137
Ridpath, George, 39
Rousseau, Jean-Baptiste: his *Le Café*, 125
Rowe, Nicholas, 136; his *The Fair Penitent*, 137
Rymer, Thomas, 37, 82

St. John, Henry. *See* Bolingbroke
Sandford (playwright): his *The Female Fop*, 96, 99
Satire: in comedy, 3, 38, 82, 101; and the attacks on the stage, 26–27, 37; and Fielding, 39–40, 40–41, 120; and Congreve, 50, 52, 54; and Vanbrugh, 51, 54; and Farquhar, 52, 54; and Dilke, 55; and Baker, 59, 61; and Cibber, 62; and Steele, 64, 84; and Addison, 97; and Gay, 110
Scriblerus Club, 83
Sentimentalism: defined, 127–28; and comedy, 127–32
Settle, Elkanah, 26; his *The Lady's Triumph*, 93
Shadwell, Thomas: his *The Squire of Alsatia*, 33
Shaftesbury, Anthony Ashley Cooper, third Earl of, 131
Shakespeare, William, 21; his *As You Like It*, 98; *Henry V*, 92; *King Lear*, 33; *The Merry Wives of Windsor*, 123; *Much Ado About Nothing*, 92; *The Taming of the Shrew*, 98; *Twelfth Night*, 57
Shirley, James, 20
Smith, Adam: his *Wealth of Nations*, 9
Smythe, James Moore. *See* Moore-Smythe, James
Social relationships: in 18th century life, 1–19, 77–82; reflected in drama, 2–3, 20–24, 42, 43–44, 48–49, 54–68, 69–76, 90–94, 121–27; in Congreve, Vanbrugh, and Farquhar, 44–54; in Baker and Burnaby, 57–61; in Cibber, 61–62, 88–90; in Steele, 63–64, 83–85; in Centlivre, 64–68, 86–88; in Gay, 108–10; in Dodsley, 110–13; in Fielding, 114–21; and sentimentalism, 128–32

Southerne, Thomas, 136
South Sea Bubble, 88, 94–96, 120
Spectator, The, 31–32, 34, 37, 79–80, 81, 83
Stage, reform of. *See* Criticism, dramatic
Steele, Sir Richard, 1, 3, 29, 32, 38, 57, 61, 81, 90, 93, 97, 134, 135; and the merchant class, 5, 32–33, 34, 38; his treatment of social relationships, 34, 44, 63–64, 75; and reform of the stage, 31, 33, 37, 38, 63; and Drury Lane Theater, 37, 38; and various periodicals, 83; quoted, 84, 94–95; and *The Englishman*, 94–95; and sentimentalism, 130–31
———*Apology*, 32; *The Christian Hero*, 130; *The Conscious Lovers*, 5, 33, 34, 38, 66, 83–85, 86, 89, 93, 131, 132, 137; *The Funeral*, 63; *The Lying Lover*, 63; *The Tender Husband*, 63–64, 74, 75
Sturmy, John: his *The Compromise*, 99–100
Swift, Jonathan, 106; quoted, 2; social conservatism of, 1, 2, 44; his journalistic campaign for the Tories, 78–80 *passim*; and Steele's *The Conscious Lovers*, 83
———*The Battle of the Books*, 37; *The Examiner*, 17, 44, 78–79, 80; *Gulliver's Travels*, 101, 107, 108, 109

Tatler, The, 31–32, 83, 135
Taverner, William: his *The Artful Wife*, 91–92; *The Female Advocates*, 91; *The Maid the Mistress*, 75, 82
Theaters: and audiences, 9–10, 15–19; increase in number of, 13–15, 102; and the decline of drama, 135
Theatre, The, 32
Theobald, Lewis, 39, 136
Tory Party, 11, 44, 78–80 *passim*, 81, 93, 95, 101
Town Talk, The, 32, 134

Universal Journal, The, 34–35, 81
Utrecht, Treaty of, 3, 10, 13, 34, 77, 78, 81, 91, 101

Vanbrugh, Sir John, 44, 61, 68, 69, 84; treatment of social relationships: 43, 44–54 *passim*, 49, 51, 53, 70–72
———*Aesop*, 70, 71; *The Confederacy*, 48, 50–51, 52, 64; *The Country*

House, 71; *A Journey to London,* 46, 70–71, 129; *The Provoked Wife,* 45–46, 53; *The Relapse,* 46–47, 48, 70–71

Vega, Lope de: his *El Mejor Alcalde, el Rey,* 111, 112

Voltaire, 26, 109

Walker, William: his *Marry, or, Do Worse,* 76

Walpole, Sir Robert, 2, 38, 101, 104, 114, 120, 127, 138; his economic policy, 7–9; and Gay's *Beggar's Opera,* 110

Ward, Henry: his *The Happy Lovers,* 122

Webster, John: his *Cure for a Cuckold,* 56

Wesley, Samuel: his *An Epistle to a Friend Concerning Poetry,* 31

Whig Party, 11, 34, 44, 77, 78, 81, 83, 85, 86, 90, 93, 94, 95, 101

Wilks, Robert, 39–40, 102

William III, King of England, 25, 77

Wit: controversy over, 27–32; and Congreve, 49–50, 69, 70

Wright, Thomas: his *The Female Virtuosos,* 56, 74, 144 n.13

Wycherley, William, 20, 90; treatment of merchant class, 23, 35; his *The Gentleman Dancing Master,* 143 n.12; his *Love in a Wood,* 23, 67